THE FROG SNOGGER'S GUIDE

D1375354

"I commend *The Frog Snogger's Guide* to frogs, toads and snoggers – all of whom have much to learn from the authors' thoughtful analysis of the basis for working relationships."

Sir John Harvey-Jones

For a complete list of Management Books 2000 titles,
visit our web-site on http://www.mb2000.com

THE FROG SNOGGER'S GUIDE

A guide to getting on with toads ...

Susan Lancaster and Sean Orford

Illustrations by Adrian Dixon

2000

First published in 2000 by Management Books 2000 Ltd
Cowcombe House
Cowcombe Hill
Chalford
Gloucestershire GL6 8HP
Tel. 01285 760 722
Fax. 01285 760 708
E-mail: mb2000@compuserve.com

Printed and bound in Great Britain by Biddles, Guildford

British Library Cataloguing in Publication Data is available
ISBN 1-85252-348-4

Contents

Contents

Acknowledgements

With many grateful thanks to:
    Diedre, Maureen and Dave – for their initial support and
        encouragement
    Sue, for her many ideas and support
    Tim, for encouragement
    Mum and Jane, for their unconditional support
    Gill, for her invaluable assistance, advice and support
    Sean and Adrian, for making Frog Snogging such a pleasure
    Denis, for his love and patience.

Susan Lancaster

INTRODUCTION

A GUIDE TO FROG SNOGGING

In this, the introduction to our book, we have decided to buck the current trend of starting everything with the phrase 'As we enter the New Millennium'.

There is a problem we are addressing in this book, and hopefully opening your eyes to, that has been with us since the beginning of time in one form or other. In its wake it has left devastation, many foundering dreams, broken hearts and lost causes. Even the thrones of the great and mighty have toppled into the dust – Charles I and Louis XVI spring to mind almost immediately. If ever there were two people who should have learned to Snog Frogs and Cope with Toads at their mother's knees, these were the chaps. Sadly their ignorance, born of their power, position and general isolation from the masses, led them to a sticky end. All the attributes of money, power and status could not prevent them losing their thrones and their heads. They failed to be effective frog snoggers and the Frogs sharpened the blade.

Frog snogging is about developing people power and positive relationships through getting to like the un-likable or snogging the seemingly unsnoggable. As the road to success becomes more crowded and much more competitive, it is very important for us to develop and cultivate business and personal relationships with the 'right' people. Unfortunately, some of these 'right' people might turn out to be Frogs you would rather ignore completely because of your intense dislike, or Toads to be avoided at all costs.

We meet many travellers on this road to success. Some of them are even more competitive than we are, some are aggressive and some are good and helpful people who will be of great assistance if we know how to contact and communicate with them. This then, is the key. We are not talking about superficial communication that can lead to all kinds of misunderstanding, but real and practiced communication that can make friends out of enemies and enable us to like the un-likable.

This guide shows the practical strategies for building the bridges that allow us to snog the unsnoggable. Closing the gap between you and your Slimy Frog is a process of wooing and courting and it often requires help and understanding. Success lies in transforming the difficult business or personal relationship so that it changes from the negative and repulsive to the positive and fruitful.

From our experience and in our own areas of work, we have needed, of necessity, to snog many Frogs. Initially, some of these Frogs we would rather have left well alone, but with perseverance in the snogging department we have found that that many of them have turned into Princes who we have even got to like. It is this process of snogging that has enabled us to reach our goals. Many Slimy Frogs who seem unsnoggable at the outset often turn into valued business contacts, acquaintances and in some cases, good friends. Sadly, though thankfully not often, some Frogs turn out to be Toads with a poisonous bite and a nasty after taste.

Successful Frog snogging begins with self-knowledge and a realistic understanding our own skills and shortcomings. We must also understand what sort of person others experience us to be. Then, we must have knowledge of our Frog with meaningful awareness of his skills and shortcomings. It is in understanding our Frog's need for security and self-esteem we are able to moderate and develop our approach accordingly to ensure that they feel happy. When we are aware of what it is the Frog needs from us, we are able to get what we need from them and this is the snogging strategy.

In most cases, we find that good and successful Frog snogging involves two willing participants working to a mutual advantage, but sometimes we have to snog with unwilling partners whether we like it or not. In the end all Frogs can be snogged, they can be seduced with the right approach as demonstrated throughout this book.

This book is intended as a general guide, to be read and enjoyed while providing some useful and lasting lessons that can be read again and again. For simplicity and ease of use, we have used only one gender when describing Frogs and snoggers although we recognise that they may be of either gender.

There are contact details provided at the end of this book, so if you would like to talk to us and discuss your experiences of Frog snogging, please get in touch. We might even be on the verge of a mutual snog. In the mean time, good luck with your journey on your road to success. Whatever your route and destination, enjoy your snogging!

Susan and Sean

1

The Story of the Princess and the Frog

Whatsinitforme simply lay back on the lily pad,
pursed his lips and waited

Have you ever needed something from someone you just do not like? Have you ever needed to be nice to someone you simply find repulsive? Have you ever wanted something very badly and yet not known how to get it?

Success in life, especially in the world of business, is invariably bound up with somehow, some way, finding a method of liking the un-likable and then being able to communicate in such a way that you get what you want. Being nice to those you would rather kick in the shins and smiling on the outside whilst seething on the inside is an art form. The process of getting what you want through making relationships is what we call Frog snogging.

Many of the people you will need to snog will be enjoyably snoggable. Some will be vile and yet the snogging must proceed. This is all well and good but we are left with the unpalatable question of how do you do it? How do you snog the slimy Frog and live to tell the tale? By the time that you reach the end of this book, you should know how.

A Variation on a Theme

Our apologies to the Brothers Grimm and our thanks for the loan of the tale, for grim and desperate the situation was.

Long, long ago there was a land many thousands and thousands of miles from here. A land ruled by a good but foolish King with a less than helpful wife. A land where those that did the work had empty bellies, empty pockets and rickets while those that ruled had fat bellies, gout and constipation. In fact the only thing that both the rich people and the poor people had in common was the emptiness of their pockets. The poor people had empty pockets because they had nothing to put in them. The rich people had empty pockets because they had other people to carry everything for them, even their handkerchiefs.

This good and foolish King had a rude and nasty daughter – 'The' Princess. 'The' because she was an only child, having no brothers or sisters. The Princess was horribly spoilt and very stuck up. She got everything she wanted when she wanted it and screamed if there was any delay. Living alone in a castle with her mum and dad, the King and Queen, she never saw the poor people and thought pockets were merely for decoration.

The castle was grand. The castle was stupendous – there were rooms that the King did not know existed. The castle also had large and beautiful gardens. There were countless servants, with empty pockets and rickets busily keeping the stately pile going.

In such a setting there was generally not too much for a stuck up kid to do other than mope around, huff, look sullen and be generally adolescent. In her frequent fits of boredom, the princess – let's call her Princess Wantalot – would wander around the grounds annoying anyone she came across. Wantalot had a rather useless golden ball that had little to recommend it other than it was made of gold and was subsequently fabulously valuable. This ball had been given to Wantalot by her grandmother one afternoon several Christmases ago amidst the jolly festive celebrations and Yuletide cheer.

The time was coming up to a good Christmassy film on television that the adults all greatly wanted to watch. Her granny, to get some peace from the screaming child, gave her the ball. With the ball came the dire warning that its value was beyond measure and that its loss would probably be followed by the loss of Wantalot's head. Wantalot sat spellbound in almost absolute silence, never heard of before, through the film and much of the following day and the day after that and, indeed, the day after that also. Wantalot took the ball with her everywhere she went, even to the bathroom.

The precious golden ball consumed all of Wantalot's attention and soon became her pride and joy. One day, even more bored than usual, Wantalot decided to go down to the pond. She had her seamstress make a soft, bright red velvet bag in which she placed the golden ball. It was this bag that she carried now. The sun reflected off the water right into Wantalot's eyes causing her to squint in a very unattractive manner and her eyes filled with tears. Unable to see where she was treading on the path, she tripped over a loose shoelace and fell. She landed with a wallop, face-down in a muddy puddle. Her precious golden ball rolled out of the bright red velvet bag and, striking her neatly on the head in an act of defiance, it rolled off down the path and it fell, plop! into a deep part of the pond.

17

Wantalot began to cry. Then the cry turned into a wail. Then the wail then turned into a scream and Wantalot generally made a three-course meal of her displeasure, complete with coffee, biscuits, after dinner mints and a rather nice amaretto liqueur.

You see, all her life she had simply to whimper and servants would appear, as if by magic, and attend to her every need. But in this situation on this lovely summer's day, no one came to her aid. Wantalot's screaming grew in volume and intensity because she just realised that the bright red velvet bag was empty and that her precious golden ball was now lost in the dark depths of the pond.

It was not too long before a large slimy Frog, disturbed by the awful racket, jumped onto the lily pad nearest to the edge of the pond to see what was going on. Now, according to the Brothers Grimm, their Frog was distressed that the princess seemed so unhappy; he cared and wanted to make things better for her. But then their Frog was really a prince. Our Frog was *training to become a toad.*

Far from being sympathetic to Wantalot's predicament, the Frog simply looked on in wonder at how amazingly stupid human beings could be. He was, in fact, rather an opportunist Frog and as usual, he was on the make, feeling that there always had to be a percentage in any situation for the taking. The Frog – let's call him Whatsinitforme – would do or get almost anything for 20% and all of anything for 50%. Whatsinitforme sat back on a lily pad and waited, feeling that a wait might be worth his while.

Wantalot began to panic and wonder what she could do about her precious ball. Staggering awkwardly to her feet, she hobbled down to the pond. She dipped her hand in the cold, muddy water and quickly withdrew it. It was then that she noticed the Frog, Whatsinitforme, watching her. 'What are you looking for?" he asked.

Wantalot was at first incredulous that the Frog could speak. Having come to terms with that one, she jumped up and down in indignation and demanded her ball back, outraged that this Frog had not thought of getting it for her already.

"Do you know who I am?"

Whatsinitforme just smiled. "Do you know who I am?" he replied. Our princess did not yet understand the rules of negotiation. In a world where you cannot demand what you want, you must learn how to get it and how to make the deal. The quicker you learn, the quicker the deal gets done. Whatsinitforme decided he should explain these basic rules of life to Wantalot. He told her that when you are a Wantalot in the big wide world, you need a Whatsinitforme to provide and ensure that you get what you want – though all the things that you will ever want will come at a price. To get what you want, you must pay the price asked.

Wantalot protested and shouted and demanded again to know if the Frog knew she was. Whatsinitforme just smiled. Wantalot stamped off and came back and went away again and came back again. In the end she stopped protesting and Whatsinitforme offered her a deal. After all, he explained, if you want anything in this world you have to pay the price, whatever the price is, even if you are a princess. After some long consideration, Wantalot decided she did want to make a deal; she did want her precious golden ball back. But, when Whatsinitforme told Wantalot the deal, she was gob-smacked.

Whatsinitforme said that he would get Wantalot her ball back (he knew some good old boys down below that lived at the bottom who would bring it up for him if he asked them – they owed him one), provided she promised to give him a big kiss. We are talking a really big kiss here, no peck on the cheek, none of this French one-side-and-then-the-other; we are talking the big snog, closed eyes, tongues and everything, the full business.

Wantalot stared in disbelief and disgust.

"You must be joking," she shouted and ran home, horrified at the awful thought of snogging the Frog.

That night, Wantalot missed her precious golden ball and she knew she must get it back. She thought of telling her parents but knew that, after the fuss she had made at Christmas when she had got the precious golden ball, she would never live it down and if her grandmother found out, there was no telling what might happen. She paced her room in despair; she demanded drinks and comfort foods from the rickety servants who ran up and down the stairs all night with hot water bottles, lemonade, chocolates and cream cakes. In the early hours of the morning, the exhausted Wantalot finally fell into a fitful dream sleep only to wake screaming every so often as she dreamed of the open mouth of the Frog descending onto her face.

19

Everyday Wantalot went down to the pond to talk with Whatsinitforme and in vain tried to get her precious ball back. Every night she stayed awake, worrying and planning. Every day she took her new plan to the water's edge. She thought there must be some way she could get her precious golden ball back without needing to snog the Frog. Wantalot tried every ploy she could think of. She offered Whatsinitforme clothes, possessions, riches and power. She even stooped to 'please' and 'pretty please' to no avail and finally fell on her knees begging. Whatsinitforme simply lay back on the lily pad, pursed his lips in the manner of one expecting a kiss – the kiss – and waited. He knew how to wait. Frogs do. A little pressure had been added to the situation when Granny had called on the telephone to say she would be paying a visit.

So it was that one week and one day after the ball had rolled down the path and ended up with a plop into the cold muddy depths of the pond, after eight disturbed nights, countless harrowing dreams, and having finally faced the facts of life and the harshness of reality, Wantalot resigned herself to her fate. Wearily she made her way down to the pond to submit to the Frog and pay the price Whatsinitforme had demanded in full. She just must get the ball back. Try as she might to avoid the inevitable, in the end, she had to face the fact that the price was the price and if she really wanted her precious golden ball back she would have to pay the price in full to get it. However, she discovered at the point of capitulation that Whatsinitforme had ideas about raising the price and she learnt that you have to keep the Frog to the deal. She got her ball back. She also discovered to her surprise that she quite enjoyed snogging and that maybe it could be fun. Not perhaps with this Frog but, as they say, there are plenty more Frogs in the pond and who knows what they have to offer.

This is not the end of our tale, though they do all live happily ever after. It is the beginning of understanding the process of life, negotiation, communication and business. So this is not a sad tale. Wantalot learnt many things during this week:

- She confirmed for herself that the price for her precious golden ball was worth paying.
- She discovered that Frogs may be slimy but they have their uses.

- She even began to like the Frog and admire some of his characteristics, such his tenacity and his strong negotiating stance.
- She developed the desire to know more about how to communicate and negotiate with Frogs, which is what this book is about.
- Most importantly she learnt that just because you snog Frogs they do not necessarily turn into princes. Most remain Frogs and, if you are not careful they will turn into Toads.

The Moral of This Story

It is true that triumph over adversity happens in real life as well as in fairy stories. In our version of the fairy story, we have a Frog whose sole ambition in life is to get his percentage, to get his price. He knows full well that the only way he is going to accomplish this is to wait – and he is patient. The Frog represents all those people you have to deal with to achieve what you want – and there can be Pleasant Frogs (the ordinary majority), Lesser Frogs and Slimy Frogs. The princess is you. You are the person who has to discover the 'how' to snog to get what you want. To be a Frog snogger you need specific skills such as:

- ➢ understanding people and yourself
- ➢ understanding the personality of the Frog
- ➢ knowing who to snog
- ➢ knowing how to snog
- ➢ grooming the Frog
- ➢ developing networks and helpmates
- ➢ developing plans and strategies
- ➢ dealing with rejection and chapped lips
- ➢ dealing with bad breath.

Whilst some people may have inherent snogging ability, most snoggers are made, not born, and learn the hard way. This need lots of practice. In these enlightened times, we find princes and princesses chasing Frogs, actively seeking the perfect business relationship and kissing as many Frogs as possible in building their businesses. Frog Snoggers develop their skills through hard work. We apply all of these methods of Frog snogging in our own, everyday life in order to obtain our desires and ambitions. Snogging can become something you will enjoy when you begin to find what it is you are looking for. Our Frog Snogger then, is the person climbing the ladder of success and cultivating other people on the way up who are going to help him or her meet the chosen goals.

2

The Slimy Frog and Lesser Frogs

*The academic reluctantly
promoted to managerial status*

There is nothing quite like a good snogging as even our nasty Princess ultimately found out! A good snog can drive you wild, it builds on itself urging you to much more uninhibited explorations! In the extreme it can also be a comforter or it can just bring two people very close with a togetherness that makes you feel absolutely cherished and protected. At the same time it is also an unspoken commitment to one another for whatever reason and for however long. Great – isn't it? Especially when you end up getting into the joy of uninhibited exploration leading to a deeper involvement.

But do we want to go this far in the snogging adventure with a Slimy Frog or even a Lesser Frog? Perhaps not, but we do want to achieve the same outcome in a business sense. The Slimy Frog will appear regularly throughout this book and he is the metaphor for some one for whom we exhibit definite negative feelings – and yet he is someone who we must learn to like even to the point of snogging if we want to get anywhere in our quest for success and recognition.

Slimy Frogs

A profile of the Slimy Frog may be a composite of a number of different traits, but not necessarily all the traits at the same time. Let's have a look at a couple of possible examples of these different Slimy Frog characters, as they appear to us.

- Firstly there is the **large, domineering forbidding character** that, upon first encounter, does not encourage any feelings of warmth or rapport. In fact, the person wishing to extend friendly overtures towards this character will be repelled at every turn. He tends to ignore people completely or talk down to them, and does not tolerate any kind of 'new thinking' or initiatives that do not bode well for you, the Frog Snogger. It is likely that this Slimy Frog could be in a position of influence and rank (having arrived there with the excess baggage of self-opinion, ruthlessness and ambition). He has no time for greater or lesser Frogs and is not disposed to help anyone at any time.

- Second is the Slimy Frog character we know as the **pleasant, communicative type** who says one thing and does another and in truth is a clever manipulator. You think you are getting along well with him, but then have doubts because you find yourself being manoeuvred into a situation that you had not anticipated. These Slimy Frog characters are always trying to get you to do something totally beneficial for them and with no benefit to you. However, the whole process is so subtle that on many occasions you don't even know it is happening. You begin to positively dislike the 'phoney-baloney' he puts on during conversations and the over friendly attitude that shrieks of 'beware the Slimy Frog!' Nothing is believable and yet, because of his skills, it is.

- Our third Slimy Frog character could be the **academic reluctantly promoted** to managerial status but really doesn't want to know that he now has to accept responsibilities – he is much more interested in the technical side of his work. He can project as the 'dilapidated tramp' uncaring about his appearance and sloppy. He can have long, unkempt hair that accompanies a permanent scowl. He is not beyond going to a board meeting and producing a pair of ladies tights in lieu of a handkerchief! He really does not want to exist in the real world and therefore tends to be a law unto himself. His non-conformity makes it extremely difficult for you who, to a point, have to respect convention and be seen to be conforming in order to succeed.

All day could be spent adding or deleting character traits to the profiles of the Slimy Frogs depicted above and creating new Slimy Frog profiles (one of which could be the Slimy Frog you have personally encountered), but for the time being we will stick with the above three examples.

As mentioned above, you, dear reader, may find that the Slimy Frog you have to deal with is a different breed altogether – but still a Slimy Frog in your perception. To demonstrate this point I will tell you about Mary.

Mary was quite young and naive but also ambitious. She was an administration officer with high hopes. Together with a highly qualified senior executive secretary, she worked for the Chief Executive Officer of a large company. As it happens, he is not unlike our first slimy Frog, and as far as Mary was concerned, he earned his name. He always communicated with his senior secretary in a pleasant and friendly manner, while hardly ever addressing Mary, preferring to communicate with her via his secretary. Of course, the more this went on, the more he became the most horrid, gross, Slimy Frog for Mary.

The day arrived when the senior secretary was called out of town to help a family member who suffered a severe accident. This left Mary at the mercy of Slimy Frog – horrors! The CEO was all-powerful, remote and feared by many people because of his position and he was not a good communicator. Mary struggled, thankful at being left alone for most of the time. However, the inevitable happened – he was having an important meeting and wanted Mary to arrange this meeting in his office.

Mary knew very well that for the number and status of these people, the boardroom would be a much better venue for the meeting. Somehow she summoned up enough courage to tell the CEO this. Politely, Slimy Frog said that the meeting would be in his office as originally planned, but when the guests arrived he too realised that the more appropriate place was the boardroom. He then instructed Mary make the rather time-consuming transition to the boardroom. This she did capably and efficiently whilst, at the same, time keeping the guests happy. Later, after the meeting was concluded and anxious to rectify the matter, Mary managed to explain why she had suggested the boardroom in the first place. This was the turning point in their relationship. The CEO immediately respected Mary for voicing her opinion. He was so used to people kow-towing to his every need and opinion that it was like a breath of fresh air to find someone who did not.

Was this Chief Executive Officer really a Slimy Frog, or only in Mary's eyes? It didn't really matter. What did matter was that Mary found the ability and courage to snog the Frog by believing in herself and the correctness of her decision.

Lesser Frogs

As well as the variety of Slimy Frogs mentioned above, there are also Lesser Frogs who are Slimy Frogs in the making, might even be tadpoles or some form of pernicious spawn. Yet in the context of doing business with them, or just developing genuine feelings for them, they can present as much as a challenge as the Slimy Frog, especially en-masse. They are representative of the rather decent, helpful individual, but with one aspect of their character which immediately puts a person off the idea of developing any kind of relationship with them. These negative characteristics in the Lesser Frog could include such things as:

- outbursts of rage for no apparent reason
- arrogance, making him quite oblivious to other people
- a plodding, mild-mannered and/or procrastinating Frog who is

incapable of making a snap decision – infuriating and difficult to deal with because you have to abide by organisation rules and regulation which seem to hold our plodding Frog in a straight-jacket

- enjoying stirring up dissension among his team or other staff
- ultra-conservatism which renders the Lesser Frog resistant to any kind of change and totally uninterested in bolder steps
- defiance and bloody-mindedness making for an untrustworthy Frog
- a tendency in a managerial position to be overpowering and dominating
- the secrecy that can, on many occasions, prevents maximum productivity from being achieved by yourself or anyone else, by withholding information.

Obviously, some of the above character traits may not have been recognised or dealt with before this Lesser Frog was appointed to a managerial position otherwise he could not have attained such a position. Other personality disorders that may have been well hidden before promotion could include antisocial behaviour, mild schizophrenia, paranoia or excessive emotion. Self-centredness may be triggered after attaining a position of authority. Added to all of the above are the inevitable personality clashes that happen when people are so alike they cannot agree or are so opposite that they never agree.

Of course, we can choose not to deal with either the Slimy or Lesser Frogs, but there are times when we need to promote ourselves and we really have to learn to like these un-likeable characters because they may be instrumental in our own promotion to the higher echelons. If we choose to cultivate these people, then it will be by accepting them as they are. We are not setting out to change them in any way because we know full well that people only change when they want to change. No, we are simply hoping to establish a rapport with them so that they can help us and in so doing, be helped in return so that a friendship of sorts is established.

Another example of horrible slimy Frogs may be customers of your business. You may have snogged all the Frogs who needed to be snogged to establish yourself in business, but there are still more

Frogs, both benign and slimy who you need to snog in order to stay in business. These are the nit-picking customers who are never satisfied, the customers who are always driving you mad because they want a deal so low that it is undercutting any kind of profit margin. These are the customers who are satisfied with your product or service in the shop, but the phone never stops ringing with complaints when they get home. These are the customers who are abrupt, rude and demanding. These customers are the true Slimy Frogs, but they also keep coming back again and again to purchase whatever you have to offer. They recommend their friends who come and make significant purchases. They are pure gold for your business.

We all have customers or clients of whom we say 'not him again!' when we hear that they have made an appointment to have their hair cut or their car serviced. No matter how tempted we are to suggest that they take their custom, their irritating idiosyncrasies and their constant complaining elsewhere, we know that we must keep both their custom and the other custom they may bring in by word of mouth. So the snogging must go on and in these cases we must either conquer or tolerate Slimy Frog because we cannot do without him.

Obviously, most of the Slimy Frogs and Lesser Frogs outlined earlier have what *we perceive* to be huge problems, but I am sure that if you asked them what their problem was, they would not be able to tell you because they imagine themselves to be perfect. In fact, they would never see themselves as any of the characters we have listed above and would see themselves as kind, well meaning individuals who cannot be bothered with some aspects of their lives, which can include good communication! In fact, they may see communication as an unimportant issue.

You may well ask at this point how the Slimy Frogs got to their various levels of management or executive posts and positions of authority or influence in the first place. They did exactly what we are suggesting that you do – they started to like the un-likable even if the un-likable in their assessment may have been very different from your perception of the un-likable. Like you, they knew that they needed certain people to help them progress. If the Slimy Frogs found that people with whom they wanted to negotiate were anathema, then they made it their responsibility to take the necessary steps to like the un-likable because they wanted to move themselves forward. In fact, if the truth were known, they still get along quite well with their promoters. Once a camaraderie or communication level has been established, people tend to remain on a friendly basis with people who have helped them.

We must then accept that any problem the Slimy Frog and the Lesser Frog may have is his problem and it has absolutely nothing to do with us. Their problems exist for a variety of reasons, none of which are of our making. For that reason we need never lose any sleep over them or indulge in any inferior feelings which would affect our communication abilities.

Attitudes

When we do not get along with someone else it is, of course, his or her fault – no question about that! But is it really? Are we in the large majority of the people who blame others and circumstances for their own misfortunes and failures? It is not only how we see others but also how we see ourselves. We cannot hope to befriend any type of person or come to like the un-likable without knowing ourselves thoroughly, warts and all, and having the confidence to communicate with other people.

In tandem with developing our own self-knowledge and confidence, we also have to take a look at our attitudes when we communicate with other people. We have attitudes that determine within ourselves how we perceive other people and due to these attitudes, more often than not, we make snap judgments based on first impressions. This is why first impressions are so important. If a good first impression is created, then most of the alarm signals that shape our attitudes towards people are disabled and we become much more relaxed and receptive towards strangers. However, if the first impression is not so good, then our alarm systems remain on guard, making it much harder for us to be receptive to the individual concerned. This, of course, becomes a vicious cycle because the person we are communicating with senses our tenseness and remains up tight.

Let us say that a Lesser Frog, Freddie, is the person with whom we are doing business. Freddie's hair is a little long for our taste. Freddie is not the tidiest person in the world and Freddie has an irritating habit of sniffing with every other word he utters. He also sports a remarkable amount of his breakfast on his tie front, as though he is saving it for later. Unfortunately, we have attitudes about long hair, sloppy appearances, breakfast on tie and, especially, sniffing – so you can see where that tends to leave Freddie. Out in the cold!

This may be an extreme example, but is serves to demonstrate how both Freddie and ourselves are starting our relationship at a distinct disadvantage that need not have arisen. We are up tight and on guard, transferring all our negative feelings to Freddie and his tie. Our pre-conceived attitudes are therefore placing any further relationship between Freddie and ourselves in jeopardy. This is bad news for Freddie and for us as our personal feelings prevent us from understanding him, seeing beyond our prejudice and being a little more receptive.

The majority of us have attitudes both positive and negative, about other people's characteristics and traits and unless we can deal with these attitudes they can, and do, put many relationships at risk. In fact, it is these attitudes that must be overcome when we are dealing with Slimy and Lesser Frogs.

When We Open our Mouths and Speak

Let's return to the snogging scenario at the beginning of this chapter and take a deeper look at the snogging business from a romantic point of view. We snog because we want to snog. We do not make judgmental decisions before we decide to snog, such as:

? I hope she is not thinking of wedding bells!

? Can I handle the fact that she is smarter than I am?

? I wonder if she has thought about going on a diet?

? Can I put up with the way she is dressed?

? Can you smell those armpits?

No, it is a human psycho-chemical impulse of the moment, which drives us to snog because we have an unconscious feeling that it is right to do so. It is the natural progression of the relationship so far and we want to register our understanding and empathy with our partner. We are unabashedly drowning in our emotions and letting it all hang out without a care in the world. Our bodies do the talking, because this is the only way we can transfer our feelings from one to another at this time.

We like to think that we were created to treat each other equally, to get along with each other equally and to communicate with one another on equal terms, which we can do quite happily while snogging. In both our personal and business lives, the trouble starts when we have unclear minds and closed mouths.

Time and again, when some one is asked which is the greatest difficulty encountered in a new business start-up, the reply is invariably and not surprisingly, getting to know people and contacts and developing same. It would appear that we are all looking for the elusive ability to get along with people and cultivate those people so they can and will help us. So we have to understand that we need to communicate verbally and snog with people we don't like and overcome these attitudes of ours which are encouraging negative messages.

In the purely romantic snog, we don't give a hoot about equality, attitudes, differences or anything else – we just want to get on with the snogging and more! In the business snog we certainly don't regard ourselves as equal. We harbour all sorts of pre-learned attitudes, and differences that tend to be blown out of all proportion. *These problems are thus created by ourselves and not by other people.* Do I hear a gasp after reading this sentence? But is it absolutely true – even in a situation where the other person is patently wrong, it is entirely up to us as to how we perceive and deal with the situation to our advantage. The responsibility for getting the business snog right is squarely on the shoulders of the snogger.

If you are having difficulties establishing a rapport with someone, you need to clarify each and every situation with them and ensure that they understand what you have been saying. This is where the real understanding and communication is needed. One of the most complex problems we encounter in communication is the ability to express our thoughts clearly and have our listener understand exactly what we are saying. Over a period of time we need to ask ourselves regularly if:

- we are relaxed and calm when we express our thoughts, or are we hurried and short
- we think as we deliver the message
- we choose a clear, succinct method of delivering our message
- we are at peace with ourselves because if not, that very soon rubs off on the other person
- are we sending out any negative messages.

There are a number of things we should be guarding against.

🔔 Trying to overpower the other person with words rather than taking time to really listen and gain understanding through listening.

🔔 Ignoring the feelings of someone who is perceptibly nervous or unsettled, and instead of giving him or her a sincere smile and some support during the conversation, we walk away pretending not to have noticed – and say nothing.

🔔 When trying to solve arguments, do we do it with a clear head and calm words or do we use harsh words and stir up anger? Always remember that the resolution of an argument must always be a win-win situation for both parties.

🔔 When we are making plans, especially if they involve other people, do we seek advice and guidance or do we think that our way is the best and only way?

🔔 When dealing with the un-likable, do we respect the fact that the other person at first sight may not be what he appears to be and that if we seek and find some understanding, it will draw him out and a chink in his armour may appear?

🔔 Being judgmental or accusing the Slimy or Lesser Frog if he has done us no harm, but keeping an open mind.

Reviewing the above may temper any prejudice we might harbour towards our prospective Slimy Frog. If we are going to progress in our career, we have to deal with all these things many, many times over. How we deal with them is up to us, and our ability to learn from our experiences is dependent on how well we know ourselves – a subject we will touch on in greater depth in the next two chapters. In the interim, we should remind ourselves that it doesn't matter who we are or what we are, we all have been given eyes to see.

People Need People

John Donne said 'No man is an island' and this is as true today as it was 400 years ago. Whichever way you look at it and however much you may try to ignore it, people need people, no matter what their circumstances. While this is true in every aspect of our lives, it applies particularly to our career paths. Yet many still find it difficult to communicate and network.

As you can appreciate, we are going to bump into Slimy and Lesser Frogs on a regular basis whichever way we turn and therefore it would be wise for us to start thinking how we can like the un-likable – people we would not normally choose as associates.

Some of us may be able to take this in our stride but, for most of us, having to get along with someone we don't like creates enormous problems, not the least of which is lack of self-confidence in dealing with the situation.

In our business lives, we meet people who are mentors, advisors, confidants, guides and coaches, helping other business people to meet their career or business goals or just to do just a first class job of work. It is important for us to cultivate these people in order that they may help us. In tandem with building our own self-belief, we can enlist the help of a variety of managers or business contacts listed above as chaperones that can help us with our task of snogging with Slimy Frogs and Lesser Frogs. Examples of how these people can help are listed below:

☑ *A person who has a contact who has a contact.* You may have a very good friend who knows someone who knows the Slimy Frog quite well. This contact could be particularly helpful when gathering information about your Frog.

☑ *A manager who can be cultivated to pave the way for you.* You might be on friendly terms with a manager in your organisation that can engineer an introduction and informal meeting with your Frog.

☑ *A fellow businessman.* If your Frog is an entrepreneur, then a fellow businessman who knows both of you may step in and become the catalyst for your relationship with Slimy Frog.

☑ *A senior professional career person.* Someone who may have had dealings with your Frog and know the best way to approach him and will guide you accordingly.

Never be afraid to ask for other people's help because there will undoubtedly come a time when you will be in a position to return the favour. You will find that by and large professional and business people will want to help and they will stick by their commitment to you.

3

Snogging Personality Types

The various personalities involved in relationships ...

Understanding People

Successful Frog Snogging has to start with the ability to understand the various personalities involved in the relationship. The participants of the snogging relationship are just like the ingredients in a soup. When they blend well and compliment each other the flavour is fabulous. When ingredients clash, are too sweet or too salty, no one wants it and there are lots of leftovers. The ingredients of the snogging relationship include you and the Frog plus any lesser Frogs and the environment or market place in action at that time. People in relationships and ingredients in soups vary in type, flavour and texture.

In this chapter, we would like to introduce you to the eight personality archetypes.

The two major steps in frog snogging are about understanding the person you wish to snog and understanding yourself, your needs and your style. By understanding both yourself and the frog you will increase the effectiveness of your frog snogging dramatically.

The Parts of a Person

Just as we are all composed of the same physical components, we are also composed of the same psychological components. We define these psychological components as being social, intellectual, emotional, spiritual, mental, intuitive and creative. The make up of our physical components vary so that people are tall, short, fat or thin. Likewise, we also have differing psychological components.

For example, someone might have a well-developed chest or powerful shoulders – they might also have a well-developed emotional drive or a powerful conceptual drive. The physical body is easier to read because it is there for us to see, but with a little practice, it can become just as easy to read the psychological body.

- The physical body is built from biological tissues and the personality body is built of psychological attitudes.

- The physical tissues are built from components of skin, bone, muscle and fat and the psychological attitudes are built from components of thinking, feeling and doing.

- All our physical tissues have specific functions in enabling our body to operate and process food into energy. The psychological components have specific functions in enabling our inner being to operate and process our experiences in conscious understanding.

Just as exercising the body builds the outer person, exercising the mind and the emotions builds the inner person.

The three psychological components

- The *thinking (T) function* is about how we think about what we feel and what we do. It forms that basis of our moral codes regarding our behaviour and our sense of right and wrong, plus the ability to order events in a logical way. There are also components of memory and authority associated with this function.

- The *feeling (F) function* is about how we feel about what we think and about what we do. Emotion is the basis of empathy, sympathy and understanding of self and others. There are also components of self-esteem, recognition and the exercise of power associated with this function.

- The *behavioural (B) function* is about how we act and react to our thoughts and feelings. This function is body dominated and when it is activated it is either immovable or unstoppable.

For example, Josephine is *thinking* about Napoleon and what a nice chap he is. Her *feelings* are a riot of warmth, longing and desire and they distract her from attending to everyday events. Her *behaviour* is to become irritable, have a fluttering heart, become physically aroused, be off her food and snap at everyone until she meets her loved one in warm embrace. Napoleon is *thinking* about Josephine and just what a sexy lady that Josephine is. He is *thinking* in his daytime thoughts and in his dreams of how he can hasten his meeting with Josephine. His *feelings,* like Josephine's, stop him being rational and although his irrationality may not be enough to lose a battle, they are enough allow him to forget everyday things in a state of romantic amnesia. His *behaviour* is increased energy that leads him to fight that day with great fervour and win battles outright.

We talked about the shape of attitudes in individuals in the previous chapter. These attitudinal shapes vary as some are dominated by thought, some by feeling and some by action. In all of us, this thing we call our personality is built from the building blocks of our attitudes. How do these functions of thinking, feeling and doing relate to you and your plans for your networking development? Are your strong points thinking, feeling or doing?

Types of People and Frogs

Understanding the essence of other people and frogs and how they operate is a continual process of learning. There are many clues that we can learn over time, such as dress, body shape, stance and gesture, and also the way that people use language. Over many years, in order to understand the rules by which others function, we have asked many people the following three questions:

Who are you?

This gives us insight into other people's thinking. It is their self-concept and it describes how they see themselves. It is the logical rules by which they live, the moral structures that govern their behaviour and attitudes. It also shows the memory, or lack of it and the ability to organise and structure time and tasks. The clarity and power of the answer to the question 'Who are you?' will show the person's inner authority.

How do you know people like you?

This gives us insight into the world of other peoples' feelings. It shows how individuals wish to be treated by others. It tells us about the person's ability to be empathetic and sympathetic. It tells of their sensitivity, or otherwise, to ambience and the feelings of others. It shows the edge of intuition and the ability to act spontaneously on hunches. Some people who have lost touch with themselves and others will be unable to answer this question at all.

What makes you feel comfortable and secure?

This gives us insight into the world of other peoples' actions and behaviour. Because we all structure our lives to enhance the things that make us feel comfortable and to naturally avoid those things that represent threats, our patterns of behaviour describe our need for security and the maintenance of that security. A person is telling us how he or she acts in order to maintain feelings of safety and how they will act when threatened. Personal bias or prejudice should never interfere with our attitude when considering the answers to such questions because the things that create security or threat for you may seem ridiculous to someone else or vice versa.

When wooing Frogs and attempting to find out how they operate, it is important that the Frogs should always feel that you treat them with some degree of positive regard, even if it is not unconditional.

So, how do we identify the answers to the above three all-important questions? We hope you will be able to answer them after reading about the following eight main personality types outlined as follows.

Before continuing, just a word about the 't.f.d.' initials in the left-hand column of the definition panels. As indicated previously, the (t) is thinking, the (f) is for feeling and the (d) is for doing. The dominant factors are shown in capitals.

Type One – Physical type (tfD) THE DOER

TYPE	Who are you?	How do you know people like you?	Where do you place your security?
Physical t | f | **D** **DOER**	I am a solid body and I live in a physical world. I know that I am alive because I can experience it through my senses.	Be physical, punchy and to the point. Don't use long words and fancy ideas. Tell me now and tell me like it is. Most importantly, do what you say when you say you will. Touching and sex.	I am secure when I am healthy, feel vital, potent and dynamic, and a match for the task in hand. **Insecurity:** Intimidation by a stronger person, being made to look weak or small.

The attitudes of this type are dominated by the physical need to do. When presented with the *'Who Are You?'* question, this person is likely to look at you as though you are mad. Their own awareness of, and identity with their body is so strong that they think you must be joking. "What a stupid question! You can see who I am because I am standing right in front of you."

We also find that the sense of liking and being liked is dominated by the sense of touch. This is a hard form of touch that might include grabs or punches and has nothing to do with the softness of stroking. Handshakes are aggressive and the person will make judgements

about you by the nature of your handshake. Security is dominated by shows of potent action, with the ultimate insecurity coming from being shown to be weak and to lack potency. It soon becomes clear when talking with this physical type that all their attitudes are body dominated. In terms of the three attitude components, this type has a configuration of little thinking represented by a lower case 't' and, little feeling represented by a lower case 'f', but with lots of the doing component represented by the upper case 'D'. Thus the attitude configuration of this type is 't f D, behavioural.'

Implications

If you consider for a moment the world of someone who is physically dominated, then the body and matters of the body dominate their entire experience. Food and drink are important, exercise and sport is exciting to either take part in or watch.

The ultimate physical experience of touch is sex, which is often rough and aggressive. In a world dominated by the body and touch, it is hard to touch someone much closer than during the act of sexual intercourse. For the body-dominated person, the doctor, the ultimate body fixer, is god. Body-dominated types live in a short time scale and have a demand for instant action. They easily become restless, have problems relaxing and would rather be doing something. They often show little patience with others and can have a short fuse.

Type Two – Social type (tFd) THE BELONGER

TYPE	Who are you?	How do you know people like you?	Where do you place your security?
Social t **F** d **BELONGER**	I am a member of my family, my workplace, my club and society at large. This gives me my identity.	Make me feel included but give me a non-threatening time. Talk to me about the weather and the price of frozen chips. Take some control, show me and lead me. Sensual stroking.	I am secure when I am accepted, when I do not have to make decisions or take responsibility. **Insecurity:** Exclusion from the group/team, being sent to Coventry.

The attitudes of this type are dominated by feelings. They want to feel that they belong. They live in a world of 'us' and groups. This person tends to put experience 't' and drive 'd' on the back burner. This can lead to a feeling of a lack of personal responsibility, as the emotional drive to act is not tempered by thought.

When responsibility is not considered at the thinking level, the simple emotional reactions, 'It is not my fault', or 'It's all their fault', prevail. These people act in and live in groups and feel the strength of their numbers.

When asked *'Who Are You?'*, they will identify themselves as belonging to a group. The smallest group is the family that might be simply a husband and wife. When a person answers the question by putting their group membership first they belong to this type – 'I am Mr or Mrs ...' or 'I belong to/am a member of/play for/dance with ...'.

Belonging involves being accepted and acceptance demands that they do not threaten the group in any way for fear that it will reject them. To avoid threatening the group, they must show they belong to the group through conforming to the group norms.

Controversy within the group is to be avoided. Generally the rules of least resistance are adopted so they don't discuss sex, politics or religion in this house. Their attitude to life is 'don't rock the boat'. Liking is about being made to feel that they belong and security comes from the feeling of belonging.

Group bonding involves lots of 'stroking and grooming'. Just as monkeys sit communally and remove each other's fleas, groups sit and stroke each other's egos and are often sensually tactile. Insecurity is in not being allowed into a group, of being excluded or rejected by that group or in not belonging.

Implications

The implications of this need to survive through process conformity leaves people unable to make decisions without group backing. This particular area of human consciousness is known, in politics, as the 'silent majority'.

For the economic machine, they are the cannon fodder of the advertising campaign. To the politician they are the people who have the ability to dramatically change the expected outcome of an election when

41

they all move and vote as a body. All groups are led. Among the drivers who lead these groups are the tabloid media, trends, fads and fashions.

Type Three – Intellectual type (Tfd) THE EXPERIENCER

TYPE	Who are you?	How do you know people like you?	Where do you place your security?
Intellectual **T** f d **EXPERIENCER**	I am the sum total of my experiences. I enjoy new experiences and change, but I could easily become bored and have difficulty with commitment.	Stimulate my intellect and give me exciting ideas. Make me feel that this relationship is novel, unique and like no other one that you have ever had. Argue, be contentious and stretch my thinking.	I am secure when I am not tied down in ideas or actions and when I am free to experience the new and novel and when involved in change. **Insecurity:** Routine, boredom, controlled - unable to express thought and feeling.

The attitudes of this type are dominated by thinking 'T'. This allows them to play with their mind and be intellectually superior. The weakness of both feeling 'f' and action 'd' leads them to become the armchair experts that can hold forth on any subject. These people can be found on chat shows and panel games.

People who lack the Experiencer's sharp wit are often fooled into believing that this group of people does actually know what it is they are talking about. Those that make the mistake of acting on such shallow advice are often disappointed later. This general lack of grounding due to the dislocation from both thought and feeling leaves these people in an airy state unable to make commitments and keep promises.

In answer to the question '*Who Are You?*', they are just as likely to shake their heads and tell you that, as they and life are forever changing and developing at such a rate, it is impossible for them to say just who they are. Liking comes from the shared experience of the novel and the new and the subsequent ability to discuss and argue about it.

The thinking component can lead to debate and mind games, which are hard for other personality types to keep up with. When thwarted, this same razor sharp intellect can be turned into a whetted knife in the form of cutting sarcasm. Security is in maintaining the freedom to think and act independently. Insecurity is in being stifled by routine and order.

Implications

These types are bright. They have good and inventive ideas and are able to break down the tired and outmoded attitudes and practices of the past. They can argue a point and always have a new angle or view on events. However, they have difficulty with follow through. Ideas are easy but action is difficult. The most difficult act is that of commitment. They are fickle and tend to have a butterfly mind that move from one pretty flower, one interesting event, to the next. They are ultimately inconsistent and cannot really be trusted in long term planning. These people could often have problems with emotional relationships and become philanderers or serial monogamists.

Type Four – Emotional type (tFD) THE POWER HOUSE

TYPE	Who are you?	How do you know people like you?	Where do you place your security?
Emotional **t F D** **POWER**	I have a strong sense of me and mine. I would like to be recognised as an exceptional individual. I use the force of my personality to maintain my position.	Make me feel that I am the most important person ever - that I am special and exceptional. Make sure you know my name and never confuse me with anyone else.	I am secure when I have the power to do what I want and others recognise my right and need to do so. **Insecurity:** When not recognised, when devalued or faced by bankruptcy and bigger egos.

The attitudes of this type are dynamic and powerful. They have all the energy of emotion 'F' combined with the ability to act 'D'. Unlike the Experiencer, this personality can make things happen and see things through. However, they lack the very essence of personality type three – the insight of thought 't' into the consequences of their actions.

When asked '*Who Are You?*', they may be surprised that you do not know who they are. They normally come over as seeing themselves as pretty special and if you do not see them that way now, they are sure you soon will. They will answer the question with a simple but powerful 'me'. They will tell you that they are their own person, self-made and self-motivated, but it becomes apparent that they protest just a little too much and actually need your recognition for their achievements.

For many of these types, the only way they will know that you like them is if you offer such recognition. They will show they like you by sharing some of their power with you. This may be in the form of gifts, money or knowledge. But however much they give you, remember they have lots more in store.

Security comes from the exercise of power. Power has many different currencies – it maybe money, influence, knowledge, possessions or emotional dominance. In a more general sense, most business people whether working as a street trader or for a multi-national organisation, are driven by this need for power in the market place. Insecurity is usually in the form of needing to deal with a bigger ego or the loss or threatened loss of their power.

Implications

Because this personality has an almost pathological need for power and recognition, they are the most difficult to deal with. Almost all disasters are the result of this driving force running free and unstructured. In their relationships – both business and personal – the power-balance and the need for recognition will affect everything.

Type Five – The Mental Type (TfD) THE ORGANISER

TYPE	Who are you?	How do you know people like you?	Where do you place your security?
Mental T f D **ORGANISER**	I am a thinker and do not express my emotions easily. I like order and I expect to have my authority respected.	Respect my position and listen to what I have to say. Do not interrupt me - you will get your turn. Be clear, precise, organised and punctual. Do not go back on your word.	I am secure when life is organised and predictable, when those around me are constant and dependable. **Insecurity:** Loss of face and status, disloyalty, emotion, irrationality

Thinking 'T' and doing 'D' dominate the attitudes of this type. For this person, feelings 'f' are held in check. This means that emotions and feelings are greeted with fear and are to be avoided at all costs. In answer to the question *'Who Are You?'*, this type will tend to indicate that status is important and that loss of status is to be feared. Status and position are important in how they want you to see them and how they see themselves.

When the 'dustman' becomes a 'cleansing officer', we know we have just entered the status driven world.

In these personality types, there is the ability to sidestep emotional responsibility. Processing cognitive thoughts into action without due regard to the emotional implication of that action to either yourself or others is described as duty. There are many people in many jobs that exist by doing their duty. When challenged about their actions, they will tell you that they are simply doing their job. It can be difficult to have a relationship both business and personal with this personality type because there is a tendency to feel emotionally disconnected. However, in the right place, doing their duty means a reliable and faithful partner.

Dominated by a sense of thinking, these types become good planners. Their fear of emotion and the irrational makes them feel secure only when everyone plays by the rules. Whereas the previous emotional types tend to dominate the world of entrepreneurial business, these mental types dominate politics, government at all levels, the legal and medical professions and the church. In short they are the pillars of society who see their role as providing and policing the rules by which everyone should operate. Their concept is that if everyone plays by the rules, we all know where we stand and the world and the human condition becomes an ordered and measured process.

Implications

Rules and laws are designed to limit irrational and anti-social behaviour. Limitations on the freedom of emotional and intellectual expression create fixed attitudes that become traditional and unable to bend to the current need. Because of the reliance on past fixed traditions, there is a tendency for this type of person to look to past history in an attempt to respond appropriately to current events. This process can lead to fixed and rigid thinking processes and attitudes.

Type Six – The Intuitive Type (TFd) THE VISUALISER

TYPE	Who are you?	How do you know people like you?	Where do you place your security?
Intuitive T F d VISUALISER	I am quiet and have a feeling for atmospheres and situations. I do not like to be forced into expressing my opinions without deep consideration.	Be quiet and sensitive. If I need to face issues, let me do it slowly - do not be too pushy or aggressive. Give me time to express what I need to express without talking over me. Always listen to what I say and give it weight.	I am secure when I feel I am in tune and going with the natural flow of creation, when my world is full of harmony and beauty **Insecurity:** Disharmony, hatred, violence, negativity, aggression and hurt.

The combination of thinking 'T' and feeling 'F' enables this personality type to have great insight into the thoughts and feelings of others. However, with a severe lack of the doing function 'd' these people have many problems in attempting to put what they feel into action. When asked the question *'Who Are You?'*, this person may take a long time in answering and when a response does finally emerge, it will be along the lines of feeling that he or she is 'part of the cosmic whole' or 'a small drop in the ocean of life'. It soon becomes clear that these people feel a connection with the force of nature in its most spiritual sense, but in lacking the physical drive to take action, they feel helpless to do anything about it. The result of this lack of action is a tendency to withdraw into themselves in an attempt to avoid the difficulties and pain that they can both see and feel.

In the extreme, these types will withdraw from the world altogether into small communities of like-minded souls in monastic type settings where they can pray, meditate and visualise a better way of being and generally avoid the pain of everyday life. These people seek places of solitude and peace and will work hard to create harmonious and beautiful living spaces for themselves and others.

If they do take up some kind of work with the needy and

distressed, it will be on the basis that they are able to retreat to their own place of safety to recover. Processes such as meditation and visualisation are techniques for reaching just such a space within the mind and those able to use these techniques are able to live in an internal quiet space when all around them hell is breaking lose. Security comes simply from there being no threat and insecurity from feeling threatened.

Implications

These personality types have a great deal to offer and very little opportunity to offer it. The easy access they have to both thinking and feeling makes them a perfect balance for the previous two personality types.

In the right place in an organisation or business, these people are able to offer insight into the implications of long-term plans and/or mediate in both internal and external negotiations. In western society, these personality types are generally sidelined as meaningless to modern living.

Type Seven – The Creative Type (TFD) THE INSPIRER

TYPE	Who are you?	How do you know people like you?	Where do you place your security?
Creative **T** **F** **D** INSPIRER	I am whoever I want to be whenever I want to be.	Be what I want you to be. Inspire me, give me energy and then let me use it and give back my creation. Be careful how you receive it and do not reject my work.	I am secure when I am turned on and inspired. **Insecurity:** Comes from the fear that my inspiration has dried up and that I will no longer be able to create.

Here we find our balance point, a personality who is able to see cognitively what needs to be done, is emotionally committed to ensuring that it happens and has the physical drive to see it through.

Asked the question '*Who Are You?*', the response is truly creative, 'I am who ever I want to be'. When thinking '**T**', feeling '**F**' and doing '**D**' are in balance, things can be achieved and dreams realised. These are the scientists, inventors and artists that fill our history books. These are personalities that are driven by the desire to be creative or to discover.

It is these personality types that have led mankind into the industrial and technological age. In the world of arts, they are the great painters and composers. In the world of philosophy, they are the great thinkers. In the world of religion, they are the great spiritual icons. In the world of politics, they are the great leaders. In the world of power, they are those who are able to inspire others. In the world of business, they are the great entrepreneurs that change the landscape in which we all live.

Security in the drive is the joy in the creation or discovery, the achievement and fruition of a long held image. Insecurity is in being unable to create or inspire and in feeling useless.

Implications

The ability to be really in touch with the creative inspirational centre has the potential to be totally powerful. However the ability to create leaves us with a choice to create either good or evil. Think of Hitler and Ghandi, Genghis Khan and Mother Teresa, who used the same inspirational force to motivate thousands, if not millions, of people to follow and adhere to an image of their creation.

Type Eight – The Withdrawn Type (tfd) THE FANTASIZER

TYPE	Who are you?	How do you know people like you?	Where do you place your security?
Withdrawn t f d **FANTASIZER**	I do not want to be anything or anybody. I wish to be left alone.	I do not know the answer to this question. I doubt if anyone likes me.	I have no security. **Insecurity:** My insecurity is increased when I am forced to face reality.

This personality type has ceased to think '**t**', feel '**f**' and, do '**d**'. They are withdrawn into a secure world of fantasy. When asked the question '*Who Are You?*', they will probably look blank. If you are able to get a response they will tell you that they do not have a clue. Many people described as 'mentally ill' or having an 'emotional breakdown' are in this segment of the human personality. Some are born in it and stay forever. Some are just passing through. Most of us will visit this area from time to time if only for a few minutes. Some people are here because of the medication given them to help cope with some emotional disturbance.

These types of personality can seem very disconnected and at the end of a very long tunnel where they can hardly hear you. They have retreated into an inner fantasy where all is well and good and they can come to no further harm.

They often reach this state after traumatic events that cannot be faced. Sometimes this is related to abuse or some event later in life over which the person has had no control such as physical torture or mental cruelty. Security is nonexistent other than within a fantasy. Insecurity is being forced out of the fantasy. (For insight into trauma and ways of dealing with it, see '*Trauma*' by Eva Roman and Roger le Duc-Bennett, Management Books 2000, 2000)

Implications

We all use fantasy as a way of coping. Imagine having a bad argument with a boss, colleague, teacher and so on, someone to whom you are unable to say what you really feel. Perhaps you would rather have punched them on the nose but you suppressed these feeling and walked away. But then you begin to replay the scene and change the script a little so that in your fantasy you told them more of what you wanted to say.

By the time you meet someone else and relate the story of what happened, bits of the fantasy have woven themselves into the real account of the event. After you have told the story a few more times, the fantasy has taken root and the account now bears little or no resemblance to what actually happened.

Having looked at the various types of people out there we next need to look at you. So, to help you to make a personal profile and a self-assessment, we start in the next chapter by asking you the same three questions.

? Who are you?

? How do you know when people like you?

? Where do you place your security?

4

The Art of Communication

Self-understanding is the key to communications

Understanding yourself, your aims, objectives, skills, strengths and weaknesses

In this chapter we want you to look at you. Self-understanding is the key to communication. In understanding ourselves, we begin to understand how others see us and have the potential to moderate our behaviour so that it is acceptable in a way that allows us to get what we want.

Do you know how you would like others to see you?
How do you actually see yourself now?
Do you like yourself?
Do you think you are attractive?
Do you think other people like you?
Do you have any idea of how others see you?
Have you ever asked anyone?

Try this exercise. Go to the nearest mirror and take a long slow look at yourself. Not in the casual way you do when you are doing your hair or shaving. Look into your eyes. Look at your nose, the set of your mouth, the lines and creases. What kind of person do you see? Is it a kind, open person or are you hard and closed? Do you think people would want to get to know this face, to give it a good snog?

Try smiling. Do you smile with your eyes as well as your mouth? If you wear glasses do they enhance the way in which you wish others to see you? If you wear make-up, does it enhance your image? If you have a full-length mirror, stand in front of it. Look at your stance and posture. Try it from different angles.

Do you stand tall and proud with a straight back or are you hunched and bent? On many management courses you are taught that your letterhead and business card is the first thing that the customer uses to build an impression of you. It does not matter how good your artwork is if you look like a haystack in a storm, or one of the Godfather's best mates. Ensure your physical image reflects the way in which you would prefer to be seen.

In the previous chapter, we mapped out eight personality archetypes. It is quite possible that you will identify with one or two of these personality types – they represent the varieties of people, and Frogs. As we go through this chapter, you might need to refer back to the basic personality archetypes. Let us start at the very beginning.

Whatever our position in life, we all have the need to communicate with others to achieve our aims and objectives. Communication (common union/to be at one with) is a two-way process. One of the biggest problems in our attempted communication is our assumption that other people will understand what it is we say, how it is we feel, what it is we do and what it all means. Sadly, this rarely happens as people may get only the main drift of our ideas and we may have to repeat them several times in several different ways before we get the message across. It is the same when we are receiving a message. We have a bias as to interpretation according to our own experiences. Our understanding of the message that someone attempts to communicate to us is dependent upon our understanding of that person.

Our experience of what we think they are telling us is coloured by our bias towards them. In short, if Tom is not the sharpest of people when it comes to money matters, I will not give much credence his bank reconciliation report. If I cannot believe the events, actions or words used by the communicator, I re-interpret them to fit my own thoughts and feelings. As noted previously, there are many things that will colour our attitudes such as gender, age, race, class, wealth and all the 'ists, 'isms and, 'ologies we have all been subjected to throughout our formative life. It would seem that the starting point of our understanding of our own part in the communication process is in understanding ourselves.

Without self-understanding, effective Frog snogging is impossible – especially getting to the point we are all aiming for, snogging the Slimy Frog. Step number one in self-understanding is in the question – Who are You?

You and the Ultimate

What do you think about this God bloke? What do you think will happen to you when you die? This is not such a silly question when attempting to understand the relationship with our self and the rest of creation. Our notion of what will happen to us after we die has a profound effect on the way in which we live, our sense of right and wrong and our general moral codes.

Those that feel that death is the end can sometimes be more ruthless, in that they feel there is nothing to lose and all to gain in the here and now. People who feel that there is an afterlife often believe in the need to be good in their present life in the hope of reaping the rewards in the hereafter.

Those convinced of reincarnation and karma, the law of cause and effect, i.e. what goes around comes around, are either keen to make sure they are not storing up problems for their next incarnation, or take the opposite view of 'I'll not worry now – I'll deal with it next time around'. Take a minute to think of your own moral codes. Is your ability to act limited by your own sense of right and wrong? What is the code that you live by? What are your limits?

Your Two Sides

Carl Jung, one of Freud's contemporaries, divided people into two groups, the introverts and the extroverts.

1. The introverts tend not to need the company of others. They rely much more on their own inner world of thought and feeling. As so much of their thoughts and feelings are internalised, this tends to lead to problems in self-expression. They often have problems in public speaking, selling themselves or pushing themselves forward. Each of the eight personality archetypes has an introverted side.

2. The extroverts enjoy the hustle and bustle of life and interacting with others. They need other people to bounce ideas off and find sharing their feeling and expressing their ideas fairly easy. Extroverts enjoy performing in front of others and running courses, or doing presentations. It is easier for the extroverts to sell themselves and push themselves forward. Each of the eight personality archetypes also has an extroverted side.

The following Table demonstrates each archetype and a sample of one of their Introvert/Extrovert qualities attached to that archetype.

ARCHETYPE	Introvert qualities	Extrovert qualities
Physical Doer	Immovable object	Unstoppable force
Social Belonger	Shy wall-flower	Socialite
Intellectual Experiencer	Researcher	Anarchist
Emotional Power-house	Empathiser	Dictator
Mental Organiser	Second in command/supporter	Politician
Intuitive Visualiser	Meditator	Preacher
Creative Inspirer	Artists, writers, musicians	Leader
Withdrawn Fantasizer	Fantasizer	None

Are you and Introvert or an Extrovert? In reality most of us are probably a mixture of the two and our reactions may vary from one event to another.

Your ego state

We should also consider the ego stance that we take in relationship to other people's egos. Eric Berne, a psychoanalyst, developed the theory known as Transactional Analysis. Berne considers that within each of us there are three ego states Parent, Adult and Child (Games People Play, 1964). At any one time, one of these three is dominant.

The parental part within us is that part which creates our sense of moral behaviour. It is the control mechanism that says 'ought, should and must'. As with all parents, this part of us can be authoritarian, dictatorial and fixed or warm, caring and nurturing. Berne defined these as the 'critical parent' or the 'nurturing parent'. For most of us, we are re-running our experience of our parents or primary care givers as this internalised parent that can sit like Jimminy Cricket on our shoulder, attempting to direct our behaviour.

We also have an adult ego state that Berne sees as the processor of our experience. It is non-emotional or judgmental, working only with facts and reality.

As well as the above two states, all of us have an inner child state built from feelings, impulses and spontaneity. Depending on our upbringing, the inner child may be free to play, interact and enjoy life, or be damaged, scared and withdrawn. The interaction of these three ego states within us creates what Berne called our 'script'.

It is this script of how we see ourselves that creates our perception of who we are. It also describes the stance we take when we interact with others, but it is important to realise that in interacting with others, whatever your personality type, both of you will communicate from an ego state. For example if you are the damaged inner child and the person you are communicating with is a critical inner parent you will feel very intimidated and powerless.

The reality of our self-concept is an amalgam of our basic personality type, our ability to be either introvert or extrovert and the ego state of parent, adult or child that we use at any one time.

As an example, a physical archetype with an extroverted damaged inner child is likely to be a physical bully, whereas a physical extrovert, with a critical inner parent, is likely to be mental bully. If the person's energy becomes turned inwards so that we have a physical introvert with a damaged inner child the result can be a person who is involved in self-harm.

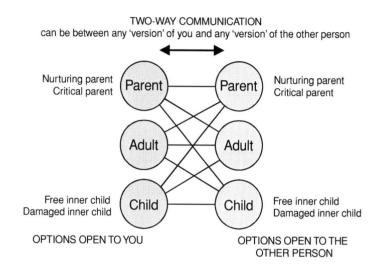

TWO-WAY COMMUNICATION
can be between any 'version' of you and any 'version' of the other person

Nurturing parent
Critical parent — Parent — Parent — Nurturing parent
Critical parent

Adult — Adult

Free inner child
Damaged inner child — Child — Child — Free inner child
Damaged inner child

OPTIONS OPEN TO YOU

OPTIONS OPEN TO THE OTHER PERSON

Consider your own ego state.

- How often are you able to communicate in situations of equality, adult to adult?
- When you activate the parental part of your ego, do you use it to nurture and care or be critical?
- When in a child state, are you free and playful or restricted, shy and fearful?
- Think about others in your life. In what situations do you become a child to the other person's adult and in what situations do you become the adult to another's child?

If you are lucky, you will be able to snog your Frog adult to adult. Sometimes parent to parent can work even if one is critical and the other nurturing. Child to child can work provided the damaged child is not too damaged and the free child has some sensitivity. As soon as the snogging becomes unbalanced with those stuck in negative child or parent states the role of the snoggers becomes more difficult.

So the questions to consider are:

- Who are you?
- How do you operate as a person?
- What is your script?
- What is it that you need to develop to make you an effective Frog snogger?

Who are you?

Look at the eight personality archetypes. Which are you? It is likely that you see your self in several. This is because we have all these components within us. We all have a body and the need to belong to social networks. We need some stimulation as a break from the boring routines of everyday life and we all have the need for emotional recognition and to exercise some form of power, however small. We all have a sense of memory, the past and traditions that define where we come from and form an ordered sense of our experience. We all have a deep intuitive side that is sensitive and insightful and we all have the ability to be creative and make things happen.

Finally we all have the need to resort to fantasy as a coping mechanism if only when watching a movie, or when we lie in bed and imagine being with the most luscious partner, or dream of murdering someone we intensely dislike. However, there will be one area that is the strongest, the one you use most often. The total picture of who you are is an amalgam of bits of all these areas put together in such a way as to create the unique individual that is you with your own tendency to introversion and extroversion and your communication stance.

If you are not used to looking at yourself in this way or if you are unsure of '*Who Are You?*', ask other people the questions about you. Ask them how they experience you. This is the 'who are you?' question the other way around. You can then compare the responses to your own inner feelings about yourself and see how they match the personality archetypes we have described.

On the next page, write down your self-concept, the way you see yourself. This is a total picture, a pen portrait of who you are. It includes all the good bits and the bad bits. Just imagine the Martians have landed. In attempting to understand these weird things called human beings, they ask you 'who are you?' How do you explain this event that is you. How do you describe yourself to a complete stranger? How do you see yourself? The more honest you can be with yourself now, the more effective you will be in the future.

WHO ARE YOU?

(Use this page to describe your self-concept, how you see yourself)

Know yourself and know your Frog

Just as you have a self-concept, so does the Frog. If you can develop a clear understanding of your own self-concept, then you will begin automatically to have a clearer understanding of where your Frog is coming from. Thus you will become a more effective Frog snogger. Appreciating the inner world of your Frog forms the respect on which the snogging relationship is based.

Liking and disliking

Imagine a continuum, which has hate at one end and love at the other. In the middle will be the point of complete indifference.

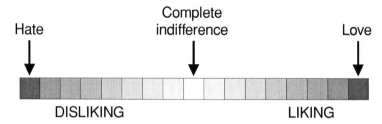

Consider these questions:

? How do you know when someone likes you?
? How do you show someone you like them?
? How do you show someone you dislike him or her?

To be liked is to be valued, to be given importance. Liking moves from indifference towards love in some way, although there is a difference between liking and loving. For many people, loving is an extreme form of liking. Disliking moves from indifference towards hate and while many of us will admit to loving, few of us will admit to hating. We prefer to change it to 'intense dislike'. Liking is difficult to fake. A person gets a sense of genuinely being liked because it produces the right atmosphere between two people. The pretence of liking never feels right because that inner warmth is not there.

Consider the archetypes. Where do you fit? What do you need people to do to show you that they like you? Look around at your friends, what is it that makes them your friends? What do they do to show you that they like you? If you are brave enough, ask your friends what it is you do that makes them feel you like them?

Write down here how you know when other people like you. What is it they have to do to show you? Also write down how you show others you like them

HOW DO YOU KNOW WHEN PEOPLE LIKE YOU?
(What is it they have to do?)

HOW DO YOU SHOW PEOPLE YOU LIKE THEM?
(What is it that you do?)

Ensure that your Frog feels accepted

As a result of the above exercise, you will realise that successful Frog snogging comes from allowing the Frog to feel accepted and valued just as you need to feel accepted and valued. Your Frog should feel that you like him. This is called getting the 'pitch' right. Tailor your message so that the Frog can both hear it and feel it. The more you are familiar with the exercise you have just been through, the easier it will be for you to be empathetic towards your Frog.

What makes you feel comfortable and secure?

It is impossible to act freely and creatively unless you feel safe. This is most difficult for critical adults and damaged children. Although there are times in some business negotiations when creating instability and insecurity in your Frog is a valid negotiating strategy, whenever possible, you should maintain a situation where you and your Frog feel secure. It is also important to realise that our securities are intensely personal, as are those things that threaten us. Objects and situations of threat are often irrational. When someone is scared of a spider, the logical argument is that the person is a million times bigger and could crush the spider with the little finger. It is not like that from inside the fear. The illogical fear is that the spider has all the power. When we examine our own fears from inside, this is true for all of us. Threats are real.

Our security strategy in life is designed to avoid us needing to face our fears. It is therefore possible to understand a person's security base by looking at what they do with their life. Behaviour and security wherever possible will run together. If you look at people who are out socialising as much as possible, always are with their friends or down at the pub, we know that they continually need to be in the company of others and that they will be threatened by isolation.

- Social extroverts with a free inner child will be gregarious socialites.

- Social extroverts, with a damaged inner child will require lots of attention and reassurance that may come across as being very clinging.

ṁ Socialites who are introverted become shy and quiet as the observer on the edge of the group who says very little.

ṁ Social introverts with a damaged inner child can become negative and may talk behind other peoples' backs, a good prejudicial gossip.

What do you use as a security base? What is your area of comfort? What would threaten you most?

Under the following question, identify and write down what it is that gives you security. Having done that, think backward in time. If you were answering that question one year ago, five years ago, ten years ago would your answer be the same? If not, how has the answer changed? How has it developed?

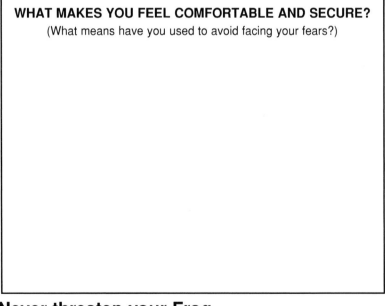

WHAT MAKES YOU FEEL COMFORTABLE AND SECURE?
(What means have you used to avoid facing your fears?)

Never threaten your Frog

Successful Frog snogging comes when you know yourself and your Frog well enough to ensure that your Frog feels valued and accepted and not threatened in any way. Create safety for your Frog by recognising what you perceive makes him feel secure.

Self-assessment

How do you feel reading back over your response sheets? If you feel a sense of well-being and confidence after replying to these questions, then you are certainly on the right track. More than likely, you feel a little disquiet and maybe need to think about what you have written. In your snogging career, you will meet many Frogs – some you will find easy to snog, others will be more difficult, and some impossible. Those that are impossible are only impossible because we do not know how to get through to them. In the ideal world, our snogging skills would allow us to get anything from anyone – even Slimy Frog.

Having completed our self-assessment, our next task is to take stock of our skill deficits. Do we have any shortfalls and if so, what can we do to improve these questionable areas. The next section is designed to help you examine your skill base and decide what you need to do next.

Personal skills and deficits audit

Although the following is a universal requirement for success, if you are ultimately going to snog the Slimy Frog, you will need to be thoroughly familiar with this exercise. Are you ready to proceed? This guide will take you through many of the stages you must define when you are searching for goals. You may well ask how this analysis relates to your ability to Frog snog? In order to appeal to the Frogs that are going to help you with you ambitions and plans, you must recognise that you have all the physical and psychological requirements to obtain the right job or contract. When you approach your Frog, you have to convince him of your eligibility and confidence. The series of questions below will give you the chance to review where you are now. You might like to come back to these questions again when you have finished reading the book. Read the following lists and mark each item with 'Yes' or 'No'

Physical

How in touch are you with your physical self? If you need to snog a physical Frog, do you have the physical energy to keep up with him? Do you possess the following:

	Yes	No
Energy	☐	☐
Stamina	☐	☐
Enthusiasm	☐	☐
Good sleep pattern	☐	☐
Good appetite	☐	☐

If you answered 'yes' to three or more of these questions, you will probably have the physical resources to achieve your goals. Less then three and you should begin to examine your life style. You may need to get some exercise, visit the gym, generally get fit, develop your sleep pattern or improve your appetite.

Social

How is your social self? If you meet a social Frog, are you able to match his social energy? Would you be happy at the pub or the club? Do you possess the following:

	Yes	No
A friendly disposition	☐	☐
A welcoming manner	☐	☐
An inclusive attitude	☐	☐
An ability to put others at their ease	☐	☐
An enjoyment in talking to others	☐	☐

If you answered 'yes' to three or more, you are probably socially well adjusted. If you are unsure about your answers, ask other people for feedback on how they see your social skills. If you have problems, it is often because you are too intense or too serious. The skill that oils the wheels of social interaction is being able to put someone at ease by having lightweight non-controversial conversations and just having fun. Loosen up.

Intellectual

How is your intellectual self? If you need to interact with an intellectual Frog, can you keep up with his mental agility? Could you argue and debate and come up with novel ideas and solutions? Do you:

	Yes	No
Communicate your ideas clearly?	☐	☐
Have innovative ideas?	☐	☐
Enjoy research?	☐	☐
Enjoy change?	☐	☐
Get bored by routine?	☐	☐

If you have answered 'yes' to three or more of these questions, you will be able to share your self-confidence and enthusiasm for your project with your intellectual Frog. If you answered yes to less than three, you are probably not doing what you want to do. Are you doing what you want to do? Should you be doing something else? Do you need to have some fun? Our intellect is the tool we use to perceive the world around us. Some people have the knack of always seeing the world in a positive light, while others maintain a negative perspective. Sharing innovative and exciting ideas clearly inspires others by getting them excited with your project. This is all so important when promoting you.

Emotional

How is your emotional self? Emotions are the powerhouse that gives us the energy to be committed to the project in hand and to ourselves. They allow us to feel good and bad, right and wrong and make instinctive decisions on a gut-feeling basis. Are you:

	Yes	No
Committed to success?	☐	☐
Self-confident?	☐	☐
Powerful enough?	☐	☐
Fully resourced?	☐	☐
Financially sound?	☐	☐

If you answered 'yes' to three or more of these questions, you are probably well resourced and have sufficient energy to see it through. Many projects fail because the resources needed for them to succeed were not available. Often this is because the full extent of the need is not understood at the outset. If you feel you are under-resourced, then take a look at your strengths and weaknesses and seek business and financial advice from experts in your field as necessary.

Mental

How is your mental self? Do you know where everything is that you need or do you waste hours trying to find simple things like sticky tape? The mental part of ourselves creates organisation and structure and time. Have you developed appropriate systems?

	Yes	No
Office organisation	☐	☐
Taxation and national insurance	☐	☐
Financial accounts	☐	☐
Business planning	☐	☐
Client contact files	☐	☐

If you answered 'yes' to three or more, you are getting organised. If not, you need to contact your local business advisory service or Business Link. Your bank manager will help you find solicitors or accountants. If you are organised at the outset, life will run much more smoothly.

Intuitive

How is your intuitive world? Do you understand the effect your actions have on others? Are you aware of the feelings of others and whether they are anxious or calm? Do you understand the effect you have on?

	Yes	No
You	☐	☐
Your family/partner	☐	☐
Your friends/associates	☐	☐
Society at large	☐	☐
The environment	☐	☐

If you answered 'yes' to three or more of these questions, you have foresight. If not, spend sometime thinking and talking it through, maybe with a counsellor or coach, about how you think your plans may affect other people in your life.

Creative

How is your creative self? How are you at solving problems? Can you see the outcome of your plans? Do you have a clear image? Do you have a clear image of your:

	Yes	No
Intended action	☐	☐
Project/product	☐	☐
Future developments	☐	☐
Various outcomes	☐	☐
Alternative plans	☐	☐

If you answered 'yes' to three or more of these questions, you must have a fairly clear image of your future development. If not, you should examine each of these questions in turn. Most importantly, you need to have other plans for consideration with alternative ideas.

In brief, ensure you are clear about your aims and objectives, that you are resourced and motivated, organised and informed. Make sure you have alternative courses to follow.

Assessing Yourself and Others

Using the questions above, it is possible to make an assessment of yourself and, to some extent, an assessment of your Frog and/or your Slimy or Lesser Frog. In all relationships, there will be an element of match and mismatch. For example, two people with similar characteristics, ideas, hobbies and so on are likely to find it easier to communicate than two people with diverse attitudes and opinions. Likewise people who communicate in a similar currency, cognitively, emotionally or behaviourally, stand a better chance of shared understanding and communication. When you snog someone who inhabits a world completely different from your own, it is you, as the snogger, who has the responsibility to go to where they are. They will not come to you. For example, if you are a thinking, cognitive type, it is no use expecting emotional or social types to be logical just for you.

You cannot make a guinea pig bark; they simply do not do it.

If you want to snog emotional Frogs, find the emotional part inside you and use it. If you don't, your snogging will fail.

To recap, it is important to realise that within us all are the three aspect of thinking, feeling and doing, our characters come from the eight archetypes, and the ability to be both introverted and extroverted. We also all have an inner adult, a parent and a child that will come into play at different times. We may have strengths and we may have weaknesses, but we have the ability to do something about out deficits if we are motivated. To understand ourselves, and the areas in which we are most comfortable snogging, we will increase the effectiveness of that snogging.

By understanding our deficits and seeking to replace them with more positive attributes, we will extend the range of our snogging abilities. Finally, in understanding our Frog, we can adapt our approach and improve our snogging. The more we understand the more effective we become.

$$5$$

Who to Snog

If the frog finds you attractive,
then sexual tension can cloud the issue

Initially, everybody! When first let loose, the snogger is rather like the child in the sweet shop. It is only when we have tried the goods on offer that we can discriminate between the good, the not so good and the revolting. We have been through our self-analysis, performed the skills/deficit audit, gained confidence and if we do not practice using that confidence so that we don't think twice about it, we will start to lose it. At the moment, you probably think that snogging is going to be like falling off a log. You are full of the feel-good factor and ready to take on the world. Unfortunately, you haven't got the experience to realise that this snogging business is far from easy to accomplish. There are little things called Frogs or Toads, who tend to put a spoke or two in any wheel.

Getting to Know You

We would like to introduce you to our hero in this case – Fanshaw – who wants to become a management consultant. He has just completed university where he graduated cum laude and is all set for his brilliant and glittering career. Well, he would be but the drawback is that, although he believes in himself and his ability to do the work, he is not a 'people person' and is lacking in social conversational skills, spending most of his time awkwardly thrusting his hands deep into his trouser pockets. You know, the kind you see at a party who is examining every book in the bookcase and every compact disc in the rack followed by every picture on the wall in the minutest of detail.

It is not that Fanshaw dislikes people. Like most of us he is quite comfortable with those he knows – once he gets to know them – but he has difficulties in the getting-to-know-you-stage. If, for example, he sees someone walking down the other side of the street that he thinks he vaguely knows and might engage him in small talk, he will dart into the nearest shop doorway or turn around and start going the other way – anything to avoid being recognised by or engaged in conversation with the individual on the other side of the road. His career in relationships has been fraught and embarrassing. It has been marked with long silences, awkward feelings and red faces with lots of 'er'-ing and 'emm'-ing. He just cannot cope with mouthing pleasantries or, scariest of all, with silences. He has difficulties finding the path that will lead to some meaningful conversation with any person, so he takes the easiest way out – he avoids people whenever he can. Not a helpful skill for management consultancy.

It is a great pity that Fanshaw does not make the effort to get to know people, because the distinguished-looking person he is nipping into doorways to avoid is actually a consultant with his own management consulting business who happens to be looking for recruits. He could have given Fanshaw valuable help and he was far from being a Slimy or Lesser Frog. We should never let the chance of a good snog pass us by.

To Fanshaw's credit, he knows that he must remedy this flaw in his character if he is to progress in his career. He knows that he has to snog, but he hasn't a clue who to snog, and he realises that it is going to be a case of finding appropriate contacts that might help him with his future career. He also realises that he has to have a plan for his career that will be essential in identifying the people he needs to cultivate and snog. Fanshaw has no doubt that some of the people are going to be Slimy or Lesser Frogs. When we mention planning, we are not talking about an in-depth business plan, but it will entail Fanshaw committing some plans and ideas to paper before embarking on the 'I want to get to know you better' phase of his future.

Cultivation Planning

Fanshaw has a very good idea of what he wants to do in life and what he wants to ultimately achieve career-wise. He knows what he wants, but he is not very sure how he is going to get it. Goals are one hundred percent necessary if you are going to do anything and get anywhere, especially in the area of Frog snogging. However, there must be a plan of action as to how those goals are going to be accomplished and this is what Fanshaw is busy trying to decide.

He knows without a doubt that he wants the following:

- ☑ job satisfaction
- ☑ to continue being a problem solver, which he really enjoys
- ☑ a certain amount of risk taking
- ☑ to be in control of his own life and not be beholden to a company clock, rules or regulations
- ☑ a comfortable lifestyle – being able to afford the things he wants
- ☑ ultimately, he wants to work when he wants to work.

Why does he want these things? The 'whys' are very important because they are the reasons which motivate us to reach our goals. Fanshaw would like a family, even thought he is currently not married. He feels that he would like to provide for this family, but he also wants to enjoy his family and spend some time with them. He also wants also to have a healthy cache of cash if things do not go the way they should and he finds himself in a fallback position. Along with all of the above, is the subliminal need for recognition and power as in Archetype Personality 4, two very strong motivating forces required to reach goals.

Having carefully mapped out his desires and goals so far, Fanshaw is now faced with the dilemma of how he is going to achieve these goals. Out comes the notebook and pencil again:

➢ First of all he must set up his own company.

➢ Second, he must set up an office.

Even at this early point, Fanshaw is getting complacent. "Easy-peasy, all this planning", he is thinking to himself. Suddenly he is hit for six.

STOP! These may be great first steps, but how is he going to do it without an income called money, without being paid for his work. At the moment, there is no sign of any work, nor is there so in the foreseeable future. He doesn't need an office or a company to be in business, *he needs people who are going to give him work.*

Hmm – he hadn't though about that. It is usually the other way round, get yourself organised first and then go and look for the work. The trouble is, he may spend a small fortune on setting himself up in business and then be left sitting at an empty desk for six months before he gets even the faintest whiff of a job or a contract. He is just fitting into the mould of every other small businessman who is starting from scratch. In the first excitement and flush of setting up your own business, or landing a very good job, there is very little further planning and least of all on the agenda is the small matter of people who are going to provide you with the necessary work, contract or assistance.

Fanshaw finally realises at this point that more than ever he is going to need people and that they are the most important commodities in business. Probably many of these people will not be his favourite type of person, and some of them, he just knows, will turn out to be Slimy or Lesser Frogs. Communicating with these species of Frogs is off-putting to say the least of it. So what is he to do?

Again, he gets down to the assessment business to work out what he has to offer which might charm a Frog or a Slimy Frog or at least get past the introduction. He has an education, is gifted in his work and is now confident, although not overly so. His downfall is people. Basically, he is a very diffident person and realises he is really going to have to work at this people issue if he is going to get anywhere. What could he, personally, offer in terms of a pleasing personality to a Frog or Slimy Frog. He has:

- good listening skills (at least he thinks so)
- alertness
- an open mind
- integrity
- professionalism
- a certain amount of empathy
- an exceedingly good knowledge of his work.

The above, he feels, is enough to make a good first impression, if he is lucky. He needs improvement in the areas of listening skills and empathy, but undoubtedly practice makes a good Frog snogger. However, he is still very much aware that if he is going to put up his shingle as a management consultant, he needs to network. This is the most important requirement, but good networking relies heavily on people skills. One thing he can do to help the networking is to write articles and letters to local newspapers and become more visible and this could lead to some introductions.

Acknowledging the fact that while getting his career organised, he had better do some networking, he ponders how he is actually going to start. Back to the list again:

- The first port of call is family and friends.

- He could join a business club, which is actively promoting business, and another club, which is connected to a hobby he enjoys – any club which would expose him to mixing with other people and help him to overcome the shyness barriers he immediately puts around himself.

- He can also start practising striking up a conversation with strangers and talking to people he meets. We only have to look at the example given at the beginning of this chapter to see the opportunity missed by Fanshaw when he decided to ignore the nodding acquaintance on the other side of the street.

- Seminars and/or workshops in his chosen field are also of great benefit in the getting-to-know-people process.

- 'People watching' is another exercise which is good for familiarising yourself with peoples' characters. Although he may not get to meet people at that time, Fanshaw can sit in an airport, a library, a shopping mall or wherever and learn many interesting character traits just by watching people, which will give him a little more confidence when approaching people in the future.

Family and Friends

As he is completing this exercise, instinctively his mind travels back to family and friends, with not very much relish. He can think of at least half a dozen Slimy or Lesser Frogs (as far as he is concerned) in his family and friends circle. Currently, the situation with these individuals is that he goes out when they come in! After getting himself thoroughly tied up in knots in finally coming to a decision, he concludes that he had better practice on a couple of these people in his 'inner circle' and see what he can do to win them around. So he set his sights on Uncle Sebastian who is loaded – he would really be a very good target. Fanshaw could never actually see him 'off-loading' on anyone but, in the long run, it might be an idea to test the generosity levels.

Then there is his 'friend' Felicia. Just the very thought of Felicia produces goose pimples of fear, rather than pleasure – still, he has to start somewhere. Felicia works for a large company that is forever having management problems. Fanshaw reasoned that it could be to his advantage to cultivate Felicia as she might provide a foot in the door for his first contract – particularly since this company is also doing a lot of work on the second stage of his university specialty.

While feeling very self-satisfied with these two choices and knowing that it is only a matter of time before he has that luxurious office, Fanshaw suddenly has a thought which is not a very nice thought and forces him back into the reality of everyday working and living. What if Uncle Sebastian and Felicia don't deliver the goods in any shape or form? He is then left without any other contacts. Something definitely has to be done about that!

At this point we feel we should mention that there is nothing whatsoever wrong with Uncle Sebastian and Felicia. They are certainly not Slimy Frogs or even Lesser Frogs. It is Fanshaw, for some reason best known to himself who perceives them to be Slimy Frogs – and therein is his problem.

- How often have we ourselves met people to whom we take an instant dislike?
- How often have we refrained from furthering a relationship because we have made a hasty, non-supported judgmental assessment of their character without even getting to know very much about them?
- How often have we denied an acquaintanceship or friendship which could have been of benefit to us in the long run just because we had pre-conceived ideas about that person?

In essence, Fanshaw is faced with two Slimy Frogs who he alone has created. Although he doesn't know it, he is not faced with the difficulty of taming two real true-blue Slimy Frogs. All he has to do in this case is to alter his attitude. When we encounter someone who we perceive to be a Slimy or Lesser Frog, we need to take an inward look at ourselves first and be scrupulously honest with our feelings of dislike.

We need to try and decide why we don't like them and if we can give any support to our reasoning. Two small exercises in the assessment of our Slimy Frog character would be to find out more about the 'potential' Slimy Frog, and also note what his role or activities have been within his business, or within the context of a large company, whichever is applicable. If, through these exercises, we manage to banish our negative attitude, then half the battle is won and we do not have a problem we thought we had with Slimy Frogs.

Defining Who to Snog

Fanshaw is wrapped in thought. Maybe he should be joining a company instead of going straight into management consulting. After all, the company could give him a lot of experience in the development and workings of business and will, of course, enhance his CV. Better still, he will meet many people there and quite possibly there will be introductions to people in similar businesses. But he would have the same problem as he has had before – if he wants to promote himself and achieve his ambition, he has to have help, so he will have to cultivate the people in the company. With careful consideration, Fanshaw draws up a list of target people who are going to help him get into this company, and vows to himself that he will master the art of Frog Snogging to get there. After all, he reasoned, if he went into the company, he would be much better placed to start his own business ultimately.

Having firmly established his career path and accepted that this most precious asset in the realisation of his plans will be people, amongst whom will be plenty of Slimy and Lesser Frogs, Fanshaw is now in a position to focus his attention on the matter of Frog snogging.

As well as cultivating people generally without a specific need or expected outcome of the cultivation, he needs to draw up a profile of the Frogs he expects to snog (Slimy or otherwise). You may question this, but it is like the drawing up of goals. When the specifications of a plan or requirement are down on paper, the image remains in your mind and prompts you each time a possible opportunity arises.

Since whom he is going to snog remains the big unknown to Fanshaw currently, he should develop some idea of what he is looking for in the person he wants to snog. To help with this, Fanshaw draws up a list of questions that he must answer and commit to memory so that he can automatically recognise a potential Frog to snog when he sees one. The answers he accords these questions will form the profile of his Frog, a profile that will change constantly in his snogging quest. The following list may help you to formulate a potential Frog-to-snog profile.

What kind of person is going to help you to get what you want?

The following questions are ones you may wish to consider.

- Do you relate better to male or female?
- What is their job/role/position?
- Are they successful, succeeding, failing, failed?
- Is their business large or small?
- What markets do they serve?
- Do they need to be located in a specific area?
- Is the person with the title the one who has the power?
- Do you prefer to deal with a specific age group?
- What about their social background?
- Is a particular academic profile necessary?
- Does your Frog have to have money?
- Are they married, separated, divorced, widowed?
- Do they have children and if so are they young or teenagers?
- What would they be doing with their spare time?
- What special experiences do they need to have had?
- What special interests do they need to have?

The above are general questions for you to work from. As you can see, the list includes questions on personal information that you should know. For example, if you have a problem communicating with someone who is much older than you, for whatever reason, it is no good your identifying an older person as a Frog to snog – you should be looking for his or her equivalent, but younger. Or, if you feel that your potential Frog should definitely have academic qualifications, then you know that the self-made Frog is not the Frog for you!

Take a few moments to list other points that you feel are important to your profile?

1)

2)

3)

4)

5)

When looking at your profile, you may find there are extremes rather than a constant norm. The profile might vary from female teenagers to male octogenarians, or be spread across social or financial groupings. This initial profile will help you to get focused but it also has to be adaptable because it will continually change over time. Most snoggers will agree that snogging people they find pleasantly attractive helps the process enormously. However, if the person is too attractive then sexual tension can cloud the issues. There can be an added problem if the Frog finds you attractive, but the feeling is not mutual.

Most relationships can involve a sexual dynamic. Flirtation encourages most relationships, even such things as buying a morning paper and passing the time of day. Frogs may be male, female, gay, celibate or whatever. Be aware of your own reactions to the dynamics of flirting. Decide how you function best and build this into what you expect in your profiling. Wherever possible, snog those Frogs with whom you are most comfortable.

Developing the profile

To continue our story about Fanshaw, he drew up and honed his ideal profile of the person who could best help him in the future. His profile reads as follows:

> A male in his forties who headed up his own business, who had been through a couple of failed businesses initially, but now had been successful with his current enterprise which was expanding and diversifying – particularly in a direction which provided opportunities for Fanshaw. Not only was his interest in squash one of Fanshaw's interests, but also this man was very much a family man with what appeared to be family values – something of great importance to Fanshaw. This man not only had power, clout and money, but he was also sympathetic to younger and bright entrepreneurs with a bit of a reputation as a kindly godfather.

Fanshaw, being Fanshaw of course, was not content with finding someone more readily accessible or a little less known – no, he had to go for the top man even though the challenge to meet this individual was somewhat daunting. However, he was convinced that if he could find a way to meet this man, he could convince him of the advantages of helping Fanshaw.

Even though he was still very much on a learning curve with the getting-to-know-you campaign, Fanshaw had now accepted the fact that it was people who would make or break him and he knew instinctively that he had a few contacts that might help him. His contacts at this point were not plentiful, but Fanshaw told them all what he wanted and they put their feelers out and came up with someone who was a member of the same squash club as Fanshaw's profile. The club was quite a way from Fanshaw's residence, but the commuting to play squash was going to be worth it in this case.

Needless to say, Fanshaw did eventually make contact with his profile and some interesting possibilities were discussed as far as diversification was concerned. The point we make is that none of this would have happened if Fanshaw had not given any thought to his profile. He would have gone on blissfully unaware that he had a few things in common with his profile, and that his profile might actually be approachable.

How often have we acknowledged that a certain famous personality could help us, but because we had no profile, we didn't entertain the idea that the idea could become reality. In fact, we didn't even give it a second thought. If we practice our Frog snogging and profiling, anything is possible.

With each snogging, you will learn. With each snogging, your ideal customer profile will develop. Do not be afraid to change and develop your personal profile, as you understand your market to a greater depth. With the profile of your Frog now developed, you should be in a position to be able to identify various managers or business people who are going to be able to help you along the way. When you begin to apply the profile of your Frog to actual people, you may well find that the people targeted are nice, ordinary people who will not be difficult to snog.

However, you may also find that one of your potential snoggees is a Slimy Frog, and there is no substitute! In this case you may well feel that the information you have on this character needs to be supplemented with additional research. Find out all that you can about your target – any personal details, individual interests, his company, how his company operates. This investigation should cover such things as:

- How long has he been in business or in the company?
- How did he reach the position he holds at present?
- Is his business growing?
- Who are his business or company competitors?
- What is the financial state of his business or the company he works for?

This information can be obtained from a number of sources but the best source will be the people who work with Slimy Frog or his company. Listen carefully to the answers you get from these people so that you can try and identify the kind of character traits or personalities Slimy Frog will tolerate. Write these down and then work out what personal assets you can bring to the situation that might help you with your initial interactions.

When you have assembled the results of this research, write down a summary and bounce this off a couple of people who know Slimy and make sure feedback from them ensures that you will capture his attention. After all, you have to convince Slimy Frog – or any Frog for that matter – that they want to listen to you and your ideas, and that they want to help you.

Having completed this exercise of just who is it we want to snog, approaching a Slimy Frog is not nearly so intimidating as we thought. It occurs to us that sometimes it would be more advantageous to pluck up courage and snog one really Slimy Frog than have to go through two or three nicer Frogs in order to achieve the same result.

6

Developing contacts

... paddling his own canoe

There are lots of Frogs out there in the pond – many are paddling their own canoe. When Frogs are working together, and it does happen, this is a network, the mutual snog. Developing contacts is Frog Snogging with someone who is not necessarily a friend, but who could be instrumental in helping you to get ahead as you seek to achieve success. Frogs need recognition for their help and achievements.

Always remember the golden rule – *if people do help you in any way, always show your appreciation and thanks.*

Never take any help for granted at any time.

As has been mentioned before and is worth mentioning again – people, need people need people ... ...! You can well imagine that if someone is going for a job or starting up a business, he or she is going to have to acquire considerable information beyond any kind of plans mentioned in the previous chapter. It is true that there is the library, the computer, the internet and many other sources of information.

However, even when we have gleaned all the facts and figures from these resources, we need someone to translate the information into reality and action – people of course. We need them because we need their assistance, if only to bounce ideas off them or to help compose a CV or to give us the name of a good accountant. Whether they be family, friends or members of the great unknown, we still need them.

The Contact Development Plan

We have mentioned briefly where contacts can be found. After that, developing contacts can be done in four relatively painless steps:

1. **Comfortable communications** – meeting and conversing with people at the very basic level either socially or on a business level.

2. **Networking** – this process is essential after mastering the first step.

3. **Cultivating your Frogs** – developing a relationship with business Frogs who can participate as a mentor, coach, helper, friend, advisor – whatever is needed.

4. **Attacking Slimy Frog** – knowing how to approach the Frog character that your body and soul rebels against.

1. Comfortable Basic Communication for the 'I don't want to', the 'I don't feel like it' or the 'I can't' novice communicator

To be really experienced at meeting, mixing and building relationships, you need to start snogging earlier rather than later which means developing an interest in people. Sometimes it can help if you approach people with the view to information gathering only. This can prove quite a motivator. This is not 'using' people although some individuals might lay a guilt trip on you by saying that it is. Rather, it is taking out insurance against the future and everyone does it. So don't feel awkward about it, OK!

Even if the contact does not turn out to be a business ally or be able to help you in the professional world, he could quite well become a treasured friend or a good acquaintance.

Following is a list of popular reasons why you would rather not be bothered to get to know other people.

Shyness	So what! Paint the worst possible scenario in your mind before approaching someone. Is this person going to kill you, hit you, bite you or lash out at you. Of course not. It is just another human being built to exactly the same specifications as yourself and therefore there is no need for you to retire into a corner like a shrinking violet.
You don't like him – His reputation has preceded him	How do you know? You have had no personal contact with him – everything you know about him is hearsay. Is that fair? No. So why don't you give him a chance? After all, you could manage one meeting and if he lives up to his reputation then you don't have to see him again. (This character is not classified as a Slimy Frog, just a 'walking reputation'.
Meeting strangers does not fall into my comfort zone	Tough – if you want to get places, you had better hurry up and get out of that comfort zone. (A comfort zone, by the way, is the place or environment where you feel supremely comfortable). You will have to do it sooner rather than later, so it may as well be now. There is no secret method of getting out of comfort zones – it is up to the individual and the necessity that drives them.

He looks so arrogant and stuck up

The best way to deal with this perception is to look at your intended contact and imagine him with no clothes on. What would be the difference then – nothing! In addition, your imagination may decide that some of his body parts are lacking in various sexual characteristics. Now do you think he is arrogant?

The Great British Reserve

The writer can recall going to a seminar once where someone stood up during the question period and asked "What about the Great British Reserve?" Coming from Yorkshire, I have only one thing to say about the Great British Reserve – Rubbish! Let's banish it from our vocabulary now. There is no place for any kind of reserve when networking, otherwise, what is the point of networking?

As you may appreciate, the reasons given above are barriers that you yourself have created. It is essential to dismiss these barriers as quickly as possible but that is usually much easier said than done. There is a requirement to know what those barriers are before you try to release them so that they no longer have any hold over you.

Once you have identified the barriers, then you grit your teeth and get on with letting go. One of the biggest misconceptions we may harbour and is applicable to all forms of networking, is that we think we are 'selling' ourselves. The process has nothing to do with selling and neither are you looking for sales leads. We are merely seeking connections and information from our contacts. If you find it hard work to keep a conversation going, always have a variety of questions at your fingers tips which may touch some hot spots and keep the lines of communication buzzing.

Without actually abdicating too much of your comfort zone, the following are simple ways and means of developing a few contacts.

Contacts

Your own family, friends and associates

Once they know that you are keen to work on building contacts and why you want to do this, they will want to help you all they can – and they can be quite valuable. You might decide to do some role playing initially and family can help with that.

You might also have an excellent associate at work who could help. Don't be backward about coming forward. If people don't know that their help is required – then nothing will be forthcoming.

A friend, of a friend, of a friend ...

This is always a good route because there is a personal contact there to begin with. It is always easier to say, "Hi, my name is Joe Bloggs and Jack Helpfulness suggested that I give you a call ... or talk to you," whichever the case may be. Somehow you are 'protecting' yourself because the onus is on your friend Jack for having introduced you.

It is also possible to 'third party'. That is to say you want to snog someone but you do not have a direct contact. Your approach might be: "everyone I meet suggests I talk to you" or " your name just seems to keep cropping up in conversations so I thought I would give you a call." You may also extend this to: "is there anyone else that you think it would be useful for me to talk with?" Keep on developing the network.

People

Make it a habit to talk to people whenever the opportunity presents itself. This again is easier if you select your unsuspecting guinea pig on the basis of his proximity to you and his facial features. If he has half acknowledged your presence with a nod or a smile, then you are away to the races. You would be surprised sometimes at the information an almost complete stranger can give you as the result of a casual conversation. If you do find an individual who can help you, don't be afraid to ask them to do so. Invariably the answer will be yes. You will never know if you don't ask.

When you manage to talk to other people, it means that you have encouraged further support for 'you'. You have held a hand out to a fellow human being and said, "Trust me!" That person immediately reciprocates which produces an optimistic feeling in yourself. It matters not if you don't get anything else out of that particular contact – they have taken the time to support you by reciprocating. That is one huge step for any novice Frog Snogger and gives us confidence to reach out again.

If you have problems keeping the conversation going through nerves or shyness, then share this fact with your new found contact. They will probably confess to the same thing and then the two of you will feel much more relaxed. If they are not as tongue-tied as you are, they will undoubtedly try to make you feel better and at ease.

Keeping channels open

Networking does not start or finish with an informative conversation. It is just the beginning of snogging. We need to keep channels open by following up with a telephone call, a lunch or a short note of acknowledgement – leaving the door open for further contact.

Communicating on the Net

Although it doesn't happen verbally, joining clubs and chat rooms on the Internet can help us gain confidence in talking to people via the written word. With continued practice of putting down written thoughts in a format which is easy for the recipient to understand, so we are training our brain to do this verbally as well.

People watching

This has been mentioned in a previous chapter, but it is worth visiting again. How many of us indulge in 'people watching'? I have to say that unashamedly, I do and I would highly recommend it to anyone else. Try and spend a total of one hour (in only minutes at a time) a week just watching and studying people in the supermarket, waiting for a bus, at the train station or the airport, on the street and so on. It can be a rewarding practice as you try and identify the type of person from body language and attitude, but without ever knowing them.

Most contacts are naturally gregarious and will help you all they can without expecting any kind of repayment. Even if the initial contacts apparently lead to nothing, one of them may just be the intermediary which provides you with the big break several contacts later.

Establishing contacts provides one of the most important aspects of a business life – visibility. The more visibility you have, the more 'known' you are going to become and the easier it will be for you to meet the people and Frogs you need to meet, and ultimately to tame the Slimy Frog.

2. Networking

I have a friend who was in the retail business. He certainly had the qualifications and personality for the job, but although he was doing good business, he was not getting the sales he was capable of getting. Why? Because he was not comfortable about beating the bushes for new clients? No, he was much more comfortable staying at home in the evening with his family. His wife used to question his sales figures. They were adequate, but she had a sneaking feeling that they could have been much more. He rationalised this mediocre figure by repeatedly telling her that he worked hard all day meeting people and doing his administrative work, so why couldn't he spend some time with his family at home. What he could not see, of course, was that if he went out to a business meeting once a week, or decided to follow up on some of his contacts at another time during the week without even thinking of sales, his output would show a marked improvement without him having to spend five nights on the road.

Many of us are like the above salesman – we don't see that the more people we meet, the better are our chances of achievement in any arena.

Do not underestimate how very important this is. It is the path of greatest resistance because, more often than not, it takes us out of our comfort zone, but it is the path that provides the greatest gains. We are all familiar with the people who are born into poverty but manage to rise above it to reach the very pinnacle of success – all due to networking.

It is our experience that you can read as many self-help books as you like but the book is not going to introduce you to the contacts you need to help you along your way and prepare you for the ultimate networking with Slimy and Lesser Frogs. It is simply a matter of people helping people and we must have people who intuitively understand our needs before they can help us – and books, no matter how informative, cannot do that.

If you still have doubts about networking, after reading the above, then think of it this way. Simplify it by likening it to a hobby you would like to take up, for example, horse riding. First of all you would like some opinions on riding from people you know or even people you don't know. You ask among your friends, your contacts, your acquaintances. They may point you in the direction of a recommended riding centre.

To make sure that you can draw some comparisons, you go to the Yellow Pages and get the names of two or three other stables that you can either visit, phone, or make further enquiries about. You may buy one of the many magazines on horse riding or better still, you may phone the local branch of the Pony Club or some other affiliated society.

All this is networking, plain and simple, nothing more and nothing less. Because this is a hobby rather than anything to do with business you will find it quite easy to talk to these people because you are relaxed. Learn how to develop a genuine interest in people and see the world from their perspective. Become a networker 'par excellence' building relationships which will continue rather than be of the fleeting variety. While you are networking, always think how you can help the person with whom you are networking and then they will only be too glad to help you.

3. Business Networking – Cultivating your Frogs

At this point, we just transfer the above actions taken to acquire information about your hobby into the business environment:

- You talk to everyone you know, and let them know what is on your mind.

- Contact any of the professional management associations to see if they have a local branch. If they do, you could arrange a meeting with one or two of the local members.

- There are professional magazines or journals – these might provide some contacts and the odd letter to a target Frog appearing in 'the press' may not go astray.

- You may wish to join a Business Group which meets on a regular basis to network amongst themselves and this organisation could provide valuable contacts and referrals.

- Snog with the local newspaper editors. If you decide to sit down with the flourish of a pen and write an article on your speciality, they could prove very useful to you. Learn the ins and outs of getting published. The odd article here and there gives you visibility and looks good on a CV.

This is networking and Frog snogging all rolled up into one.

Now we get to the subtle difference between networking for business and networking as a hobby. Psychologically we are totally unaware of the term 'networking' in our social life. All we are interested in is acquiring more information about a social event or pastime. Although we must depend on people power to help us obtain this information, we view the people involved to be of secondary importance and therefore we are totally relaxed about talking and networking with them.

When networking is applied to business, people become the primary issue and we know that our future could well ride on this one ability – to get along with them. Knowing this, means that we are not relaxed about it and subsequently the whole issue comes under pressure and this tension is transferred to other people, especially those who are our target contacts.

Acceptance of the above and the ease we acquire through the practice of basic networking can do a lot to diminish the up-tight feeling we may have when meeting business contacts, dutifully saying only what we think our respondent wants to hear because of the tension we are feeling, rather than being in a relaxed enough state to say what we really want to say and therefore encouraging the path of progress.

This can be best illustrated with a story about Elizabeth, who had everything that was necessary to become a first class executive but it didn't happen for a long time, causing her much anguish and heartache. She was too afraid, when networking, to say what she really wanted to say about how she really felt. She always put forward what she thought the other person wanted to hear and did not express her own opinions. Sometimes it is necessary for you to say what you think the other person wants you to hear, but it should also be tempered with your own views. Suppressing what you really feel could result in you going nowhere.

After some practice at networking, Elizabeth opened up and began to express her real feelings and to say exactly what was on her mind (very diplomatically, of course) and her entire career took an upward swing. People wanted to hear her views, even if they were greatly different from their own.

By now, you have become more familiar with networking and it is at this point that you are thinking back to the profiles you drew up in Chapter 5. You are now finding it much easier to identify people who can be of particular assistance to you and earmark them for contact at a sooner or later date, whenever you are ready or the opportunity presents.

Knowing your target can also help you. Is he a direct hit? In other words, has he got the information and ability to propel you to glory, or is he the link which will lead you to a direct hit. Depending on the identification of a direct hit or a link, you need to work out your timing and approach. Now is the time you will be faced with the inevitable Slimy Frog or perhaps the Lesser Frog. You cannot, no matter how hard you try, find a substitute for them – someone who is going to be infinitely more approachable. So further procrastination is not permitted.

4. The Slimy Frog Strategy

Recognising that Slimy and Lesser Frogs will only talk to you if they want to, you have to find a way of appealing to them and striking up a rapport with them. This can be done by developing a strategy, first on paper and then committed to memory, for approaching the Slimy or Lesser Frog. This strategy is divided into modules for our approach to Slimy Frog so that we can always leave ourselves in a fall back position. A typical strategy may contain the following modules:

1. Research the personal side of Slimy or Lesser Frog	What are his likes, dislikes, interests, hot spots or soft spots. What are his family and friends like and how numerous, anything else you find in your

research project, other than business. In order to build any kind of relationship we have to find a common denominator. This is essential. If there is nothing visible at work, then we must look to his off- duty profile.

2. The importance of listening

Listen very carefully to what Slimy is saying – don't listen with one ear while planning your next move. Let a genuine interpretation through genuine listening determine your next move and try to connect with people, and specially Slimy, at a deeper level. This will not come about unless you are fully focused on Slimy Frog. If you are not and you listen with only one ear while solving some other mess in your head, then you could miss the vital piece of information necessary to progress your cause.

It is a good habit during conversation for you to check in with Slimy Frog and verify the accuracy of the information he is giving you – this keeps you from nodding off or becoming distracted. Use phrases like "Yes, I understand that, but ...", "Do you mean that ...", "Could you just clarify that point a little more?" or "I don't quite understand ..."

Listening to people talk is time well spent. You are not only listening to what Slimy is saying, but you are also looking for clues which could help you to better understand him and where he is coming from.

You have already become much more sensitive and understanding with the confidence which has grown within yourself. You have honed these skills by learning to network comfortably, and now, as a final step, you need to practice listening. The more you practice the easier it will be to pick up all the hidden clues you are looking for with reference to Slimy Frog.

3. Preparing yourself for conversation

Think before you open your mouth and choose your words carefully, Are you relaxed? Have you banished all attitudes? Are you 100% focused on Slimy Frog? How is your conversation going to begin and evolve. You must not give any hint, either in your voice or with the choice of your words, that you have any difficulties with what you are saying or how you are saying it. You must now regard Slimy Frog as your friend and speak to him in that capacity.

No matter how slimy Slimy is, you don't see him as that. Your conversation must be gracious, unassuming, firm and polite, with plenty of smiles. Pretty old fashioned virtues, but they have stood the test of time and we suspect will continue to do so.

4. Give recognition where it is due

We all, every single one of us, like to receive recognition and praise. It may be difficult for you to recognise something praiseworthy in Slimy, but there is something and you must find it – even if it is quite personal. Make Slimy feel important and that he controls the situation, even if he doesn't yet know what your motive is.

5. Encourage Slimy to talk

Many of us, probably the majority, are much better talkers than we are listeners, especially when the subject matter is ourselves. Try to get Slimy to talk about himself by being genuinely interested in any issue he has raised. None of your dealings with Slimy Frog should be anything but honest and genuine – even if you perceive that Slimy is not.

6. How can I help him?

This may not happen during the first discussion you have with Slimy, but look for an issue or matter whereby you could be of assistance to him. For example, perhaps his hobby is fishing and you know a group who have just opened a new stretch of river to be fished. Bring this up, and if Slimy shows interest, offer to introduce him to a member of the group.

7. The Exit Strategy

If, during the conversation, you feel he is 'getting to you' always keep open a way out before he gets to you enough that your animosity, impatience or what have you, is going to show. Remember the regular discussions we have had about attitudes. After you leave and get yourself back together again, analyse what it was that got you uptight and work on eliminating it. If you stay, and try and continue the relationship, your attitude is going to rub off onto Slimy Frog and things will start to get difficult.

Whether it be an Ordinary, Slimy or Lesser Frog, you will find that Frog snogging is conducted over a period of time. You cannot hope to win over difficult people without first trying to genuinely understand them. It is important therefore to keep notes on who you snog, what is said, why you have to see your Frogs again and what you anticipate the outcome to be.

Keep an updated database of snogged, snogging and about to be snogged.

7

Your First Kiss

... set up for your first kiss

Look Good - Feel Good

Excitement is in the air, every day is Spring! You have worked on your self-analysis and know some more about yourself, you feel confident. You have worked hard on developing your network skills and you know when you meet someone, you leave an excellent first impression, because you are good. You have become a competent networker and you are now ready to approach Slimy Frog, full of confidence and you know that your Frog is going to say yes to whatever you ask. There must be no doubt about that, otherwise we are likely to derail ourselves before we get to the journey's end. Following our model, you have studied Slimy; you've done your research and you are now familiar with his daily routine and activities. You feel that it is now time to arrange a meeting with Slimy to set up for your first kiss. Let the courting begin.

Looking for opportunities to meet

Don't wait for a chance meeting – organise it. Listed below are just a few things you might do to encourage your first conversations with Slimy Frog.

➡ Go to a couple of meetings that Slimy attends – keep your eyes and ears open at each meeting and see if you can zero in on something Slimy says or does or does not say which may well be the foundation for a conversation. When the meeting has finished, approach and introduce yourself to Slimy before he leaves (if possible) and offer some positive comments on the issue you identified during the meeting. He may grunt, say a few words, or disappear. It matters not. You have succeeded in making a contact.

➡ If you are at work or business, you could quite easily bump into Slimy accidentally on purpose. Always have comments or conversation ready should the occasion arise.

➡ You could ask a colleague to act as an intermediary. He may be doing business with Slimy, and at one of these meetings, because of the expertise you have, your colleague could ask you to sit in.

➡ You may well be able to make Slimy's acquaintance outside work due to the friend of a friend we talked about in an earlier chapter. This friend has a friend who knows Slimy quite well, and an invitation could be contrived for you to attend the same social function as Slimy attends.

➡ The most straightforward way of attracting his attention, if you feel that now, with our help, you are motivated enough to do so, is to go directly to his office and ask his secretary, or Slimy himself, if he could fit you in for a short meeting. Explain that you would value his advice on a particular issue.

The Strategy

Trying one of the above approaches means that you have engineered a proper meeting with Slimy, for which you must now prepare. Based on that preparatory meeting, you can now gauge roughly what kind of reception you are going to get. This can be helpful in selecting modules for your approach, as outlined on page 89. When reviewing your modules, the first approach should be module 3 – *preparing yourself for conversation*. Ensure that you feel relatively relaxed about the appointment, although you may be a little up tight about having to converse with such a character – this is a bit like having some sort of jab at the doctor's. Normally you are relatively stress free, but when you have to have an injection, you get just that little bit anxious. That's okay and it is okay to have similar feelings with reference to Slimy Frog. But if you feel that you are overly tense, then back off. This can be done by letting Slimy take the floor and encouraging him with a relevant question – let him ramble on with an answer. Keep reminding yourself that the character sitting opposite to you is a friend, a genuine person. As he talks, you may find that you cannot help warming to him a little.

Because you are now sitting back and listening – then listen – as suggested in module 2. Your focused listening will be rewarded with forgetting about your initial slightly nervous state. You are already picking up some hidden clues that will be the opening for further conversation.

If Slimy does talk but confines himself to very short comments then you will have to do some quick thinking by perhaps looking around the office for something to compliment him on or you can allude back to a previous 'hidden clue' or conversation and pick up on that. Since Slimy's comments are far from flowing, such an unrelated remark by yourself would not be deemed out of place.

If you find that you are making very little headway, or you yourself are beginning to feel uncomfortable, then it is perhaps time to call matters to a halt and institute the Exit Strategy, but making sure that you leave the door open for further meetings. On the other hand, if you realise that there might not be another opportunity soon, then you could certainly try and find a common denominator that will enable you to continue the current meeting. This will depend largely on your confident ability to carry on a conversation with someone who is not being particularly helpful. It must be mentioned here that a sense of humour can often overcome mountainous hurdles. As the old adage goes, 'laughter is the best medicine'. It may just be that an injection of humour may just strike a chord with your Slimy Frog and the going becomes much easier.

> One of my perceived Slimy Frogs was a local librarian. I went regularly to the library and depended very much on the staff for their help with my research. There was this one particular librarian who was surly, uncommunicative and there was never a smile in sight. It got to the point where I used to avoid going to the library during the hours I knew that she was working her shift. Thinking about the situation, I decided that it was absolutely silly for me to avoid going to the library just because my Slimy Frog was on duty so I had better rise to the challenge and personally overcome what I thought was animosity towards me.
>
> I went to the library many times while she was on duty, hoping for a smile or a few snippets of conversation – not a hope! One day, while collecting my books together, I made an amusing remark in self-mockery and my Slimy Frog saw the humour in it. She started to laugh, the ice began to thaw and afterwards there was never a problem.

You also have to face the fact that while you might be finding the going tough, Slimy could be struggling too and he might just suddenly decide that the meeting is coming to an end with his own Exit Strategy. In this case you have very little option but to go straight to the Exit Strategy, but again, leave the door open for further talks. Whatever happens, don't push yourself on this creature, or you could quite well alienate him for good.

Always be conscious of the fact that you like this man, you genuinely like him, and that he is going to help you to obtain something you really want and he is going to become, and remain, a working partner for a long time. If you are able to adopt this attitude, you will be in a win-win situation and really enjoy every moment of the snog.

If you decide for whatever reason to adopt the Exit Strategy, then you need not necessarily feel that you must make another appointment before you leave. Another meeting is something you will no doubt engineer later, but for the moment, the best way out is to leave the door open and be completely gracious about the termination of that particular meeting. You have already established a rapport with Slimy for the next time.

Now, let us presume that you did not have to adopt the exit strategy with Slimy so we will look at another scenario. You are the butt of a slightly unpleasant remark, which is typical of this Slimy Frog. It is at this juncture that a very real possibility of sabotage looms up, which would have a devastating effect on your plans to-date.

Shooting Yourself in the Foot

So many people wanting to get ahead and be successful spend much of their time sabotaging their possible success before they get there – they shoot themselves in the foot. This usually occurs almost like clockwork, when you are on the threshold of success – as if we ourselves are willing it to happen. Usually this hijacking of your carefully laid plans comes about because you have not taken into account the emotional content of your life. You have been so busy improving yourself in other areas that somehow the emotional content was overlooked. What is needed most of all is to monitor your own moods. This enables you to identify what circumstances or actions cause these moods, and so you are able to avoid them. If you are actually able to take positive steps to do something about the issues and events which contribute to these moods, you will then not run the risk of your well-laid plans coming to nothing.

You may be at the pinnacle of success with your self-confidence and your now well-practiced ability to handle Frogs – but that demon, emotion, which you find you still do not have under control, can and will sabotage your impending relationship with Slimy at this crucial stage of the first kiss. To avoid this happening, we have to ensure that we are comfortable and in control of our emotions at all times.

As mentioned, you may be in deep conversation with Slimy or Lesser Frog only to find that they have criticised, in the mildest way, a project very close to your heart. Their remarks at once put you on the defensive and your emotions into overdrive. If you had been in control of them you should have been able to ignore this situation and carry on with focused listening. But you are not in control of them and you get edgy. Your listening becomes less focused because you are seething inside about his comments on your project – about how hard you have worked to bring it to perfection and about how dare Slimy criticise something he knows nothing about. You become more and more incensed about the unfairness of it all and less and less focused on what Slimy Frog is saying, thereby missing half of the conversation and the all important hidden clues that could be used for cracking his defence.

You are now on dangerous ground and you had better get your Exit Strategy to the fore before you make a complete idiot of yourself and lose your chance to get Slimy where you need him.

The above scenario is an example of the one side of our development, which has been ignored to date. We have to learn to cope with our feelings and that is not easy. On the one hand we have to develop sensitivity to other people, which will enable us to be empathic, on the other hand we must learn to exercise strict control over the very emotions we need to enable us to understand someone else. This can be quite problematical when we are conversing with a difficult person unless we are very practiced in the emotional restraint department.

George was an exceptionally good general manager. He had many people skills and believed wholeheartedly in teamwork. Usually he overlooked any slight aberration in staff work or routine, but on this particular occasion a team member had deliberately done something George had asked him not to do. George was livid! Instead of remaining calm, bringing the discussion to an end and then removing himself to gather his thoughts together and repress his angry feelings, he really let rip into this particular team member. In his position, he had a right to reprimand, but he did not have the right to lose his temper and shout at any member of his team. It was this incident which led to his subsequent demotion and downfall from grace.

All of the above is part of 'Emotional Intelligence', a management term that is becoming all the rage, but simply means consciously controlling our own and other peoples' emotions. Sensitivity and support for other people are the watchwords, but while being sensitive and supportive, we must not let our own emotions dominate us. This can be an extremely difficult balancing act.

We do not need to conduct an in-depth review of Emotional Intelligence with reference to Slimy Frog, but we must be aware of our emotional self and how this is going to have a direct influence on the person we are talking with, in this case, Slimy.

Our emotions always drive our decisions and subsequent actions. Our first kiss with Slimy has to be good and we have to unload any emotional baggage that may interfere with this. The best approach to this is being open-minded and in tune with the moods which can result from our emotions. The more we do this, the easier it will be to control radical and negative emotions and save ourselves from knee-jerk reactions which can cause trouble.

Other Peoples' Problems

So let us go back to the initial meeting with Slimy Frog. To recap, emotions interfered and you chose the Exit Strategy to prevent your feelings getting the better of you. Another possible scenario is that during your conversation you suddenly realise that *he* appears to have problems talking to *you*. You instinctively feel that he is having a real battle in his conversation with you and unlike the previous mention of this when he decided on an Exit Strategy he is now trying to carry on and is having a real battle to hide his discomfort. This has happened because, unlike you, he is not a networked or people person.

What can you do to make things easier for him? The possibilities for action can best be illustrated in the following story.

There was a girl, lets call her Christine, who, when she was young, moved about the country quite a bit with her parents. By the time she was thirteen, she had collected such a variety of local dialects in her speech and the spoken word had become almost unintelligible. To solve this problem, her father sent her to elocution lessons to learn to speak 'Proper English' – whatever that might be. Although she could not see the point of elocution lessons at that time, Christine attended these lessons and they transformed her career and her life both in good ways and in not-so-good ways.

Her new clear, crisp diction and pronunciation was most beneficial to her chosen career of the stage, but all through her life it was to alienate her from other people who constantly thought she was 'posh' or 'stuck-up' because of it. To her, the very people who criticised her for being posh were her Slimy Frogs and they were miserable creatures because they didn't want to know her. There was actually nothing wrong with them except their perception that Christine was too posh. This demonstrated how dangerous perceptions could be in preventing an otherwise good relationship developing.

Finally, it was her genuine interest in people that helped her to overcome this sticky problem, but it took lots of practice. Christine had put herself out to talk to her Slimy Frogs and they came round and found that she was not as bad as they thought and, surprise, surprise, actually, she was really quite a nice person. What was her secret – she asked about them and their interests – and never once mentioned her own. As mentioned in Chapter 6 – people love to talk about themselves and it was by adopting this method that Christine was able to triumph. In fact, through spending a major portion of her life doing this, it sometimes eroded her ability to speak up for herself, because she thought she would bore everyone!

In the story above, Christine had the ability understand how her Frogs were feeling – this is called empathy. You need to be able to put yourself in the other person's place and attempt to understand what they are feeling and why. In Christine's case, she knew they felt that she was a snob, that she was 'posh'. They did not want to deal with posh people for a number of reasons – probably the major one being lack of confidence and possibly fear. Having understood this, she was now in a positive position to deal with them and she started to build bridges based on the information she had learned about them. The common denominator she found would often be something personal, which could only be divulged if they were at the level of talking about personal circumstances. Once a mutual interest had been established or bonding had taken place, most of the battle had been won and after that it was more or less plain sailing, and the friendship or acquaintanceship was established.

Like the distinction between Slimy and Lesser Frogs, which can sometimes be from the sublime to the ridiculous, so can be the difference between empathies. Sometimes it is not too difficult to empathise but at other times it is almost impossible and that is where your research and knowledge of Slimy Frogs pays off.

Returning to the conversations with Slimy, you found a way of making him feel a little more comfortable by being empathic, then you also wonder how Slimy Frog views you and whether, in fact, you have made any headway with this strange Frog. In your self-assessment, you have found traits in your own character about which you are quite comfortable and happy because it suits you. You also have a good idea as to how other people see you. However, when dealing with Slimy Frog, you need to make very sure whether or not these traits you are comfortable with will be perceived as traits which cause Slimy Frog to be antagonistic and anti-you. As an example, your Frog may see you as an 'aggressive person' and you know that this is his mistake because, as far as you are concerned, this aggressiveness is nothing more than being open with people and being confident your approach. To the world at large and also to Slimy Frog, this may cause problems and you should perhaps draw your horns in a little and be prepared to try and present a stance that is a little less 'aggressive'.

The Real World

Upon review of your first kiss with Slimy Frog you feel that, although perhaps brief, it has been relatively satisfactory and you now feel that there is definitely a possibility of further meetings and perhaps co-operation. We have mentioned several ways of dealing with glitches in this first kiss, we hope to your advantage. However, if you still feel apprehensive, you could do no worse than use your imagination. You never know, you may get carried away to such an extent that you overcome all your fears and inhibitions. Even though Slimy Frog is not your cup of tea, if you can let your imagination run riot and pretend that you are physically attracted to him, you will then be able to realise how much easier this first kiss would be than the approach described above. Lets examine a possible scenario.

**The door has closed and you are alone at last with your Frog.
You both feel that this is a moment that was meant to be.
No conversation is necessary, you are alone and the
atmosphere is charged with eager sexual anticipation.
You know you will be good together and you fall into each
other's arms without a word. Bliss. The relationship is sealed
with this first kiss. When this series of actions is played out,
there are no inhibitions, no questions –
just glorious relaxation and arousal.**

If both personal and business relationships could be physical, we could forget all the tarradiddle about emotional intelligence, empathy, treading carefully, strategy, plans and so on – we would just do what comes naturally! Unfortunately, we have to come back to the world of reality with its attitudes, complicated feelings, emotional baggage *ad nauseam* and it all becomes a constant uphill battle. When we start in on this first kiss, we must recognise that trust must be built between you and Slimy Frog otherwise the relationship is going nowhere. Trust is a very important commodity. Simply put, if we don't trust people, then we don't have a relationship. Even if we are hurt, we must learn to trust and trust again, making ourselves vulnerable over and over again.

Another issue to be addressed as you enjoy this first kiss (which is going splendidly) is the matter of merging two widely different points of view. How do you do this when you are diametrically opposed? Simply steer clear of it until your relationship with Slimy is on a much surer footing and both of you are feeling confident about coming to grips with it. Then, and only then, approach with deference and compromise. More often than not, with quite a bit of brainstorming, two people can find a mutually satisfactory way forward.

We have talked quite a bit about emotions in this chapter and before signing off, we would like to suggest, as we have previously done in this book and will continue to do so, that you keep a written journal about your feelings at the end of each day. By doing this, you will begin to identify what triggers your bad or moody feelings, how you can avoid these triggers and also how you are going to deal with potential moods in similar situations.

8

Dealing with Bad Breath

Bad breath is a socially destructive characteristic

Physical halitosis – the condition known as bad breath – is a negative and socially destructive characteristic that has wrecked many a budding romance. The peculiar characteristic of the problem is that it is experienced by everyone and offends everyone except those who suffer from it. Pubs are cleared, parties brought to a close and meetings abandoned and all the while the bad-breather is oblivious to the effect he or she is having all around. It is as though such sufferers (although it is the people around the bad-breather who are really the sufferers!) have lost all sense of smell and self-awareness. While sailing happily through life, without a care in the world, they fail to notice they have just stunned an elephant at one hundred paces by merely breathing out.

It is exactly the same when the sufferer has psychological halitosis; perhaps we should call this psychological variant of halitosis *psytosis*. Sufferers of psytosis have lost all sense of propriety and can stun and offend anyone, including you, at the same hundred paces by expressing their naturally negative thoughts, feelings or attitudes. Everyone around them can sense or see the wrongness of their attitudes but those with psytosis do not have a clue.

People seldom challenge psytotics because of fearing the negative reaction they know they will encounter if they do. As a snogger, your problem is that you have to snog. If you want whatever it is that the Frog has on offer, there is no choice. You must take a deep breath, say a prayer to a higher power and proceed regardless. When your Frog has bad breath, you have to snog with a smile on your face never giving the impression that you are actually holding your nose at the same time. It is essential to just smile sweetly and get on with them to get what you want.

Always bear in mind that the one thing all Frogs suffering with psytosis have in common is that they do not know or are unable to see just how it is they appear and sound to others. They fail to realise the effect of their negative communication on those around them because the symptoms are completely out of the sufferer's awareness, as is their antisocial behaviour. Negative thoughts, feelings and attitudes are also conducted oblivious to the sufferer's awareness. They believe their problem, thoughts, feelings and attitudes to be perfectly normal and acceptable.

As an example, I am reminded of one of my psychotherapy clients who said to me during the course of a normal conversation, "You know when there are three of you in the bed and ...?" Although this was outside my range of experience, she obviously saw it as being perfectly acceptable. I held my nose and nodded and she continued with her story. In much the same way, Frogs will share their innate negative attitudes with you as though that attitude has a universal applicability.

If you confront your Frog's bad breath, the snog that was going to get you what you wanted will almost certainly fail and you will lose whatever advantage you may have gained up to this point. If you are not able to confront it, only you can decide if you are able to live with yourself. You might also want to consider that if you can 'smell the bad breath', so can others. What affect will your association with the psytotic Frog have on your future and the way other people and potential clients might view you? We all tend to suffer from guilt by association, but the most important aspect will be to keep your self as safe as possible. Be aware that if you involve yourself in the world of this Frog you may be playing outside your normal world of understanding. If you do not know the rules of the game you might get hurt. There may be a price to be paid.

Let us look at some psytotic Frogs.

The physical psytotic Frog

We all have a space around us that is ours. It is normally about the length of your arm. This is our safety space that separates us from others. For our own sense of security, we expect others to stay outside this space unless invited in. Such invitations are rarely overt. They usually involve the subtlety of body language cues, subliminal facial gestures, the way we use our posture and, possibly a suggestion of physical or social intimacy. To pick up on these cues you need a certain level of awareness and sensitivity.

Sufferers of physical psytosis do not have such self-awareness and have little or no sense of proximity. Indeed, they may want to stand close to you or touch you because that is the communication they feel most comfortable with. The result is that they stand too close and invade your ego space. For some people, this close proximity is very threatening because it triggers their fight or flight mechanisms, thus creating levels of anxiety.

I have observed interactions between snoggers and physical psytotic Frogs where the Frog takes a step forward and the snogger take a step back. The ensuing dance of advance and retreat can take them around a room several times. Then the snogger finds himself backed into a wall and the physical psytotic can now become menacing.

Psytotic physical touching can start with an unwanted pinch of the arm or buttock and then progress to actually trapping people in chairs, corners or rooms. Sometimes this behaviour can assume a sexual dimension and the recipient remains silent for fear of perhaps losing a job or promotion prospect. As a snogger, you are vulnerable.

Almost all forms of physical psytotic behaviour are bullying in that they physically threaten the victim. When involved in Frog snogging, we each have to decide what it is we will put up with and how far we are prepared to go. In these situations, the physical psytotic can see nothing wrong in his behaviour. You may be able to educate him, but in the end if you want what he has to offer badly enough, you may have to allow him to make the entire running. Your choice.

All forms of psytotic behaviour are really the exercise of power over others. This may be physical, social or whatever but in each case the exercise of power is constant. When the question is 'why do people exert power over others?' the answer is almost certainly 'because they can'. The sufferer of physical psytosis exercises power without responsibility and is totally unaware of the effect he is having on others.

The social psytotic Frog

The identity of this type of Frog exists within their sense of belonging to their social group. If you want to use them, you will have to join in with them and they will expect you to conform to the group norms of attitude and behaviour. Around the world, the normal customs of everyday life differ. These behaviours in themselves are not really psytotic as they are the normal cost of wishing to, or needing to, belong to that particular group.

It is when these practices become extreme that your problems may start. Initiation into the group may be the process of seduction, the precursor of the tables being turned on you and the Frog becoming the snogger. It may be important that you show the Frog that you belong and that you are one of 'them'.

In some groups, initiation is formal, as in the Masonic bare breast and rolled trouser legs. Less formal group initiations are witnessed in male groups, such as the army, and they can be quite violent and dangerous. Groups of women can sometimes be as bad or worse than men. In one female workforce group, in a bakery, they took great delight in initiating young male members of staff by holding them down, removing their protective garments and spreading their genitals with jam destined for the doughnuts! Normally, however, your initiation into the psytotic Frog group would only involve your attending group functions, such as meetings, meals, outings and the like. The important thing is to do what is required by the group to demonstrate that you wish to become one of them.

The problem with groups is the 'us' and 'them' situation that comes into play in the form of social prejudice. 'They' become the scapegoats for whatever 'we' see as the evils present in society, the job or whatever, at large. Prejudice leads to stereotyping such as 'all football fans are hooligans' and so on. As a recognised group member, you may be expected to join in this behaviour or be seen to condone it by remaining silent. Being prejudicial about those social psytotic Frogs who are not in the group forms the basis of every conflict the world has witnessed such as in Yugoslavia and Northern Ireland, to name but two. Sexual orientation, gender, age, race, ethnicity and religion are just a few of the prejudices – and the list can become endless.

Just remember that if you desire group acceptance, you will have to conform to the group norms. This may go against your own principles. If, halfway through your membership in a group, you suddenly decide that you don't wish to conform any longer, then you risk being ostracised or becoming a scapegoat.

A tragic result of what happens due to group influence is demonstrated by the following story.

A woman became the scapegoat in her workplace because of the size of her large breasts. As she was the butt of group negativity, she decided in desperation to have considerable breast reduction. The outcome of her decision was that she was divorced and she did not have a relationship for five years because she was so ashamed of the scarring. The actions of the group had led to this person losing her self-esteem, her marriage, her emotional life, her sensual and sexual life and left her feeling abandoned, alone and depressed.

The snogger must ask if the end justifies the means? In the end, either you belong to the group or you don't. Only you can decide how far you are prepared to go to demonstrate that you belong and whether the snog will be worth it.

The intellectual psytotic Frog

Intellectuals are engaging. When on form they can bright and shiny, humorous and witty. They have such a novel way of looking at the world that they can intrigue other people and draw them in. Taking what is the ordinary and making it extraordinary is an intellectual trick. The intellectual, who can take a motorcycle, dismantle and reconstruct it, using the handlebars as horns to look like a cow, is not being a creative artist. He is rearranging the ordinary in an extraordinary way to express an idea or make a statement. Self-expression and creative art are often confused. There is a difference between the self-expressive tendency of this type of intellectual and the truly inspired uniqueness of the creative personality.

In encouraging other people to look at the ordinary in an extraordinary way, the intellectual is also telling you that the world you live in, as far as they are concerned, is dull and mundane. The quality of being bored by the everyday experience of life, and the need to change things around them into something more stimulating, can make the intellectual an ideal Frog. The biggest problem with the psytotic intellectual Frog is that they fool you with their powerful enthusiasm into believing their sincerity in your project. Alas, you fail to see that sometimes this enthusiasm is coupled with a complete lack of long-term commitment to any course of action whatsoever. The power of the intellectual is diverted from positive action into being a tool used to argue forever about anything. The need to have just one more coffee – 'before we actually do something' – or the need to make a list or a list of lists stands forever in the way of action. The debate of 'how' and 'when' and 'why' with a side helping of 'what if?' are all ways of avoiding the deadline. The drive, concern and urgency for the completion of the project will be yours, not the Frog's. The psytotic intellectual Frog is the master of procrastination that is cleverly hidden behind diverting novel ideas, smart words, lists, statements, reports, and research.

Their need to express themselves and ease their boredom with life can lead others into taking actions that they would not normally take. For example, they like stirring things up which can lead to destabilisation that may involve going out on strike at work or staging protests. The essence of the psytotic intellectual is that they see nothing wrong in creating such levels of disruption. Having a good stir and then running away is common stance.

If you see a demonstration with thousands of people taking to the streets, the intellectual is usually the one with the megaphone, way back from the front, inciting the front line to fight on. Always ask yourself – if you were in a position where the going was getting rough, could you get out quickly if you chose to do so?

The psytotic intellectual is great in a debate but may change sides if it suits him. If you are stuck with Frogs with this type of personality, they will be great at setting things up but useless at keeping them going. If you challenge them about their lack of commitment, they may turn their intellect on you and cut you down to size using their intellect as a whetted knife in sarcasm that can be witheringly cruel.

If you find yourself negotiating with an intellectual psytotic Frog, ensure that you are protected in case he decides to up and leave your project for a more exciting one. You will need to stay awake and remain on your toes to keep up with him and survive.

The emotional psytotic Frog

Most people want to have some level of recognition. Most of us would wish to be liked. But what are you prepared to do to get it? For this emotional Frog, 'wanting' to be recognised becomes 'needing' to be recognised. For the emotional Frog, the need to be liked or recognised becomes an extreme drive. When Frog snogging this type of psytotic Frog, you must beware of the intense power of the drive they may have to become your Frog. If they feel you can offer them recognition, the drive will increase in intensity. When this is the case, the relationship becomes turned on its head. You need what the Frog has to offer and the Frog needs to be recognised to feel he is worth something. In the end, you can begin to wonder just who is snogging whom. So their need to become your Frog can be the expression of their need for your recognition.

The key to this type is the exercise of power. The emotional psytotics are really very insecure and they need to use power to enable them to protect themselves. The tools used for this purpose are mainly manipulation and the creation of insecurity in others, usually by developing fear. They demand recognition from all those around them and will go to great lengths to get it. This is not as calculating as it sounds, for most of these types are so self-centred anyway that they have little or no idea what effect they are having on others. Provided everyone does their bidding they are secure and happy.

The phrase 'attack is the best from of defence' describes this type exactly. In the United Kingdom, the general social attitude is not to complain and not to confront others. Whatever you do, don't rock the boat. This allows for a secure status quo without any emotional rationality. Anyone who is prepared to be emotionally volatile can and will threaten others. Because of the general social need to avoid conflict, the emotional psytotic Frog exercises a great amount of power over others.

In the emotional psytotic's world there is the expectation that you will respond to what is demanded, hence the jokes about 'I say "you jump", and you say, "how high?"' The question is what happens if you don't jump? In short the answer is you get 'killed'. Emotional 'murder' is not the extinguishing of your entire life, but it may 'kill' you psychologically, socially or economically. However the killing is performed, the 'death' is in the rejection. This is the very thing that the emotional psytotic fears happening to him, which is why he builds the shield of power in the first place.

The other thing to watch in this area is blackmail. Knowledge is power and can be used as a bargaining chip when needed. The idea that 'you owe me one' normally means 'I have helped you out of a situation and you are indebted to me'. The point at which that debt is called in might mean some level of compromise for you but what will the cost be if you do not return the favour? Think of the loan shark who loads all borrowings with high rates of interest. Most debts carry interest and sometimes, to the pay the interest, you need to borrow more and once you are drawn into the circle, it can be difficult to get yourself out in one piece.

Not all emotional types are bad. Some that have power also have empathy. Those that need power to feel secure may also be benevolent and are genuinely helpful. Just be careful when snogging this kind of Frog. They will need continual support, ego stroking and recognition if they are to perform for you and you may need to watch your back.

The mental psytotic Frog

Their modus operandi is a place for everything, and everything in its place. This is the world of system and organisation. If you are snogging a Frog of this persuasion, he is likely to be an official in an organisation, government agency or an official body. When these Frogs become psytotic, they are obsessed with order, rules and protocols. They are the logical types that fill the civil service, the courts and the government. For them, every decision to be made in this world is undertaken by committee, the decisions of which must be signed in triplicate, counter-signed and stamped by the lord high huff'n'puff before any action can be taken. This is the land of red tape.

Sometimes, however, all is not as it appears. A cursory scan of the eighties political life reveals a crop of mental psytotics who did not play by the rules and found themselves in compromising positions literally with their trousers down. There are also mental psytotics who take money under the counter – the bent policeman, the dodgy accountant and the rogue trader.

At their most awkward, the mental psytotics will play the game strictly by the rules, be completely unbending and allowing no leeway under any circumstances. They are so unemotional that they have little feeling or empathy for your, or any other, situation. They hide behind the desk, the uniform, the role or the title and abdicate any personal responsibility by saying, "I am only doing my job. It has nothing to do with me."

They will be obstructive and fixed and expect you to jump through all the hoops. They will not see it to be their responsibility to offer advice or help. Emotional protestation can drive them further and further into a fixed mode of behaviour. They look down on shows of emotion and emotional people as being stupid and irrational. They want you to be as logical, predictable and rational as them. They can be calculating and will think things through from every possible angle before acting. Along with the calculation comes their prodigious memory – they never forget. If you cross them they will remember the next time you need their services.

If you get involved with a mental psytotic, be ordered and logical. Present your case clearly and cogently and make sure you have covered every possible angle. Be rational and do not show emotion.

The intuitive psytotic Frog

This is probably the least likely Frog for you to be snogging unless you are involved in very specialist areas. Finding an intuitive Frog with psytosis is therefore quite rare, though they do exist. Intuitive types tend to exclude themselves from regular society in favour of quieter, more harmonious groups. These are commonly monastic, ashramic or in groups working with nature, animals or the environment. The main area of psytosis would be summed up by the phrase 'my guru is better than your guru' or 'my way of being is better than your way.' In its best sense, this area of personality has great depths of sensitivity. In intuitive psytosis there is the development of patronising attitudes and a spiritual snobbery or elitism. They tend to feel sorry for other personality types because they do not have their deep sensitivity. They look down on others and this leads the intuitive psytotic to become deeply insensitive to the world of others. They often can be smugly self-obsessed.

The guru game is interesting. There are those who get guru-itis (the frogs) and those who develop disciple-itis (the snoggers). Normally this is a reciprocal arrangement in which all parties are happy. Most intuitive psytotics start off being clean and pure. As the adoration of the disciples grows, so does the ego of the guru. If not careful, the guru starts to believe the things other people say about them and they become convinced of their own deification. Such godliness gives them special unsavoury rights – an area where the snogger does not wish to tread.

Religious and spiritual groups will often follow the group dynamics of social types with the same attitudes to inclusion and exclusion. The dynamic of two religious groups, both of which normally propound theories of tolerance and forgiveness, at war with one another, is a philosophical nonsense which would suggest 'God in on our side not yours'.

The creative psytotic Frog

Finally we are in the world of heaven or hell. The essence of creativity is the inspirational effect it has on others. The power of images affects the lives of millions. We all see and use icons in associating with the world around us. They guide our sense of fashion and music and the design of our cars and houses. Everything that we use, even the computer I am using to write this, represents the coming together of many creative images. Looking at creative psytosis depends on your point of view. For myself, I would say that the likes of Krishna, Buddha, Jesus, Mohammed, Gandhi and so on all have positive creative images. These images have been so powerful that people still follow their teachings today.

On the other side of the coin are men like Genghis Khan, Napoleon, Lenin, Hitler and so on. These images, though later generally decried after the event, inspired thousands if not millions of people to fight, kill, murder and rape all in the name of the image.

The old earth religions and the arts of white magic identified with the positive side of this creative drive. The negative side of the creative force can be identified in black magic. The parallel in the Star Wars movies is also descriptive of this, in that we all have the choice of being positive or negative.

When you hitch your wagon to that of a creative Frog, you may be heading for heaven. If you get it wrong and chose a creative psytotic Frog you will be heading for hell. Take a very good look before you leap.

9

Coping with Rejection and Chapped Lips

Was the snog just a little too rushed?

Rejection

Very early on in life, we learn to our cost about the meaning of words. There are words that open up the way we think and the things that we do such as 'yes' and 'have a go' and 'we all make mistakes' and 'you can always try again'. There are words that close things down and put a weighty burden on our shoulders and stop us doing things such as 'ought' and 'should' and 'must'. If we continually get the message that we are getting it wrong, we are indoctrinated with that little word 'no'.

No! stops us doing things. No! tells us we have got it wrong. If the word 'no' crops up in our life too much, we immediately feel a sense of guilt, whether we recognise it or not. Following on from the word 'no' comes 'can't'. With 'can't', we lose the ability to act. For as soon as we say, "I can't do that", it becomes a truly self-fulfilling prophesy. If, on the other hand, we have grown up with that little word 'yes', how much more productive we are because, psychologically, we do not have the barriers or the feelings of guilt. Following on from the word 'yes' comes 'can'. With 'can', we gain the ability to do and succeed. As soon as we say, "I can do that", we open the door to success.

People who have had extra doses of 'no' and 'can't' when they were young can go one of two ways. They can retreat into a shell so they don't have to deal with this negative world around them, as may be the case of archetype number eight, the Fantasizer or possibly type number six, the Visualiser; or it can spark a drive to press forward and get rid of the negative context as in the more extrovert archetypes. Unfortunately, there are many more of the 'shell creatures' than there are those who 'press forward'.

It is indeed odd that many people who are gifted and talented do not rise to the heights or even to a modicum of success simply because they cannot tolerate rejection. On the other hand, there are other people who are extremely successful because they have developed a hide like a rhinoceros and rejection falls off them like water off a duck's back.

Whichever category we fall into, we are on the whole terrified of rejection and, let's face it, it takes a certain and special type of person to face it on a constant basis. We are thinking particularly of sales personnel and many other people exposed to the whim of the fickle Joe Public. Even if we don't hold a 'public' position, we often face minor rejections on a frequent, routine basis and there is nothing worse than building up belief in yourself and then being knocked for six because you have been rejected.

When we suffer rejection, it is no good slinking away like a puppy who has been chastised by his master, to lick his wounds in his kennel. No, unlike the puppy, we cannot wait for re-indulgence by the person who has rejected us – we must be actively seeking the reasons for the rejection, unless it is obvious to us anyway. We need feedback, either from the party who rejected us or from someone who has been close to the situation, other than Slimy Frog, and we don't want to be shy and retiring about dealing with the issue. It is essential that we deal with the 'no' issue, otherwise we are in danger of ruining our life and turning ourselves into very negative people. This would be a disaster, because once you become a 'negative' person, it is much harder to fight back.

Don't Let It Get To You

It is easy for others to say, "Don't let it get to you." Overcoming rejection is very hard and takes practice, practice and more practice. Before we examine rejection in terms of our Slimy Frog, lets talk about other possible ways of dealing with 'no'. We say 'possible', because it is simply our contribution to the hundreds of ways recommended by other authors. The problem is that rejection is such a personal issue and sometimes difficult to deal with via the written word.

Let us imagine that you have been spending a very passionate time with the woman or man of your dreams, only to find a day or so later that she/he really doesn't want to know! The devastation! The end of the world! Why, why, why? You immediately feel that you have every right to ask him/her what has happened and why you are being dropped like a hot potato! What is more to the point, you want to find out, and as quickly as possible.

Now, transfer this scenario to the work place and your own networking capabilities. We think you will agree that you are not quite as anxious to confront your offender as you may have been in the social context. You are more inclined to go off and hide, indulge in self-pity, telling all who care to listen that it is grossly unfair and unjust! You have been rejected and unless the reasons for this rejection are patently clear to you, there is no reason why you should remain ignorant of the cause of your misfortune. Rejection could have been for a number of reasons and being able to identify these reasons will help you in the future to develop plans and approaches.

In your formative networking days, you may have felt more comfortable going in rather a circuitous route to find out why you have been rejected – asking around, especially those close to the person who has done the rejecting. Later, when you have a little more networking confidence behind you, you may want to go directly to the source for clarification.

We need to recognise that our primary tool in fighting rejection is our own attitude. If your attitude on the whole is an up-beat and positive one, then it will not be too long before you are able to handle rejection. If, on the other hand, your attitude is a bad, negative one, then you have quite a way to go and you will find it difficult to start coping with rejection. The following general action plans may be helpful in getting you accustomed to rejection. Note accustomed to it, not conquering it! The conquering is for the rhinoceros variety who are few and far between.

Getting Accustomed to NO!

Before you hear the word 'no' when you were anticipating 'yes', prepare for it. If somebody says 'no' instead of 'yes', what is the worst scenario that could come from this? If you are really keen on your contact and he implies 'no' by ignoring you, you are going to be downhearted and frustrated, but you are slowly going to emerge from this state of affairs, feeling better and with some lessons under your belt. Part of the healing process is to communicate with your contact and to find out the reason for the 'no'. If you do not, many serious reasons for the rejection are conjured up in your imagination. More often than not they are the wrong reasons, as it could turn out to have been for something simple like your contact did not like the way you spoke, or you were too pushy. Lack of knowledge on your part could wreak havoc with your plans. The knowledge obtained by you results in two possible actions.

- You are either going to cope with the rejection and then resolve to overcome it, or
- you are going to decide that it is not your problem and that

your contact is missing out on the best thing since sliced bread – so forget him.

Whether you are disappointed or defiant, in the long run you have turned around the situation to benefit you and this has been achieved primarily by communication with your contact.

There is, of course, the third possibility – that your contact will either ignore your request or refuse to tell you why he has rejected you. In that case, cut your losses and move on. We realise that this is a very simplistic statement in the minimum number of words. Another advisor or specialist in the field might have taken three or four pages to describe the process, but it still amounts to the same thing – move on. If you think ahead about the possibility of rejection and decide on your course of action if this should happen, then you are half way to dealing with it rather than letting rejection get the better of you.

Coping

In the Chapter describing our first kiss, one of the situations we encountered with Slimy was when he decided to criticise your project or idea. His attitude really upset you and you felt spurned and rejected to the point, you will recall, of opting to use your Exit Strategy. Let's imagine a couple of rejection scenarios.

Scenario one

... you have just left Slimy's office, quite rattled. You had done your homework on Slimy and you knew what he was like, so you should have anticipated his criticism. You should have realised that you were going to be one of the many recipients of some kind of snide or nasty remark from him. Knowing that you are not the only person who has suffered or will suffer makes it much easier to cope with any rejection which comes along. However, a delicate balance must be maintained in this situation because in no way should your thoughts on anticipating trouble become any form of negative thinking.

The results of your anticipatory thoughts or actions will tend to dispel any feelings of disappointment very quickly once you get outside the door. Your confidence will be restored because when you re-examine your project, you will know that there was no reason to take exception to it and that this was one of his ploys to bait you as he has done with many others.

Scenario two

Another scenario using this same first kiss scene, is that you have not anticipated what Slimy would say and that, therefore, when it actually happens, the feeling of despair over his rejection is much more acute Never mind, when you get back to your office, take a good look at yourself. What has happened to you because of what Slimy Frog said – are you still standing? Are you going to give up your efforts and forget about trying any more? Has your opinion of yourself done a 180 degree turn? Does it spell the end? Of course not – none of these things has happened. You are actually exactly the same as you were before you went to see Slimy.

Even if you have a case of mild, rather than acute, rejection, you should still conduct a post mortem on what happened and how to cope with it.

Post scenario

Rejection has been meted out – analyse how you feel and learn from this for the next time.

- Did you prepare yourself for the the appointment with Slimy sufficiently?
- Did you make sure that your interest was genuine?
- Were your responses to any questions he had asked confident enough?
- Did you really listen properly?
- Were his remarks justified?

The examples of rejection we have used provide three positive outcomes:

- You can learn to anticipate.
- Whatever form the rejection takes, you do not go through any immediate bodily or psychological metamorphosis into some downtrodden and bedraggled person. You are still very much 'you'.
- Your analysis will confirm any weak spots you may have and you can subsequently work to improve them.
- Finally, if Slimy's remarks were not justified, which is usually the case, then you will know for the next time

Just recognise that in Slimy Frog's case, the problem is all his and it has nothing to do with you, which again makes life much easier. However, going through the above exercises and getting everything down on paper will help you to feel much better.

Again, we encourage you to put pen to paper and WRITE EVERYTHING DOWN. Write about your rejection, why you think it happened and your analysis of it together with what you feel you can do to prevent it happening in the future. If it does happen again, how can you better cope with it. When you write things down, strangely, other thoughts and concerns you may have disappear and the very act of writing helps you to become much more focused and able to express your 'negative feelings' about rejection where they belong – out of your mind. The image of words on paper will remain with you for much longer than mere 'mental' notes.

If, long before you reach the point of targeting Slimy or Lesser Frog, you find rejection overwhelmingly difficult to accept and know that it will affect you badly time and time again, then perhaps some coaching or counselling will help. This can work wonders, especially if the therapy chosen involves role playing. A short course, a minimum commitment, and you will get to the point where you feel that you can go out and accept negative situations without them having any affect on you, and so reap the dividends of your new-found ability.

Chapped Lips

You could quite well be in a position where you have not only been rejected, but you have chapped lips because you really have been snogging like mad to work Slimy over onto your side, plus one or two Lesser Frogs and they are still not convinced. It is all turning out to be very difficult work and at this point you will be tired and fed up and you are totally uninterested in snogging or rejection – then take a break to regroup. Look after yourself, do something entirely different, something you really enjoy and forget about your single-minded frog snogging quest. After your break, you can return to your snogging project with a fresh mind and perhaps renewed vigour!

Self re-assessment

When you feel ready to snog again and before rushing into another session, let's step back for a moment and ask the following questions?

? Are you still committed to see this quest through to the very end?

? Do you still feel that you deserve what you want?

? Have you got a good structure in which to continue your drive – in other words, self-discipline?

? Are your goals worth the pain?

After you have looked at these four questions and can still answer 'yes' to all of them, then you are ready to start again. You are beginning to feel a slight fondness for this crabby Slimy Frog. Why does he not reciprocate? How can you find a chink in his armour? Ask yourself the following questions and make some notes beneath them for future reference.

➜ What was bad about this snogging? (What did I get wrong?)

➜ What was good about this snogging? (What did I get right?)

➜ Why am I having so much difficulty in winning over Slimy Frog?

➜ What do I need to do differently next time? (How can I improve my technique?)

Having re-assessed your position you might be in a better position to judge what you should be doing next. You may have reached the point where you want to entertain some other approaches. For example:

Hit Him Between the Eyes!

Look for a way of turning the situation around so the Slimy and Lesser Frog are so impressed with your approach they cannot do anything else but agree with you. Not easy, but you may find that if you put forward a short, well thought out, highly knowledgeable proposal, and make the presentation as passionate as you can, you completely take the wind out of his sails. He will have to admit, privately to himself, that there is definitely more to you than meets the eye. You have gone several notches up in the opinion poll of Slimy Frog.

Find A Matchmaker!

When you are worn out, tired out and fed up, then consider using some help from a third party to keep you on the straight and narrow. They can encourage you in your efforts and sometimes act as a catalyst in bringing you and Slimy Frog together. This third party could be a friend, a mentor or a coach or a work colleague.

The Too-Hard Hit!

Was your 'snog' just a bit too rushed, were you too haphazard in your communication technique rather than being structured and sensitive? Go back to your analysis mode with the above questions in mind. If you feel that the analysis confirms the description above, then you should set your sights on being a little more cautious in future encounters.

Slow Seduction!

Slow seduction is a pleasurable experience as opposed to being too keen and quick and fumbling which can make those you are snogging feel under too much pressure. Are your time-scales reasonable? Do you expect to seduce at the first meeting, or can you slowly cast a spell over a series of encounters, which is ultimately going to make you totally irresistible. Remember that slow and steady wins the race.

Many snoggers have various positive attributes that they might deploy in the seduction of Slimy Frog and this is an ideal situation for the individual who uses charm in abundance. It is also a good situation for the snoggers who feel that they have the attributes of empathy and understanding and most of all it is an optimum method for those blessed with patience.

He Is Not My Type!

Finally, there is the 'Not My Type' kind of person. What was your gut feeling about the Frog you talked with? Did you feel that you could have formed a business relationship with him? Did you feel comfortable with him? Did you 'gel'? If not, then are you on the right track? Rejection can be positive and save you from a serious mistake. You may not feel happy at all about your snogging with Slimy and your gut feeling is that the relationship is going nowhere; or maybe you are not prepared to take any of the risks outlined in Chapter 8 – Dealing with Bad Breath. Perhaps then it is time to withdraw and look for another method of getting yourself past the next rung on the ladder. Note, we recommend that you only come to this decision when you finally feel that there is absolutely no chemistry there or that the risks of furthering the relationship are too great.

It could very well be that in spite of your genuine interest, Slimy is an awkward customer and has deliberately set out to thwart you at every turn because he doesn't want to be bothered with people. In a case such as this you can rise to the challenge and pursue the relationship to the bitter end, and it could quite well be a bitter end, or you can withdraw and find another target.

We feel that the above situation is unlikely if you have acquired, through reading this book, a genuine interest in Slimy or Lesser Frogs. Eventually they will succumb to your basic honesty and good nature, especially if you can praise and help them in any way. Your positive and good attitude will help pave the way for you. However, there are cases when no matter how clever you may be at cultivating people, a particular Slimy Frog does not want to be cultivated and has absolutely no interest in you. Accept this situation, if it is the case, and move on. To demonstrate this, the following is the story of James and Morgan, two bright-eyed professional junior managers seeking the help of one particular Slimy Frog. In both cases they were essentially decent genuine people, snogging a particularly unlikeable Frog, but both feeling inclined to rise to the challenge – and pursue the relationship to the end.

> In James' case, his Frog ended up conning James into believing that he, Slimy, was the 'genuine article'. He even suggested that they work on a joint project. To James' horror, Slimy ended up being thoroughly nasty to James, giving him as rough a ride as he could. Slimy was utterly miserable and vindictive for no apparent reason.
>
> James, fortunately, was up to any challenge and he fought it all the way. He always looked for alternative methods to meet the impossible goals the miserable Slimy thing had to give him. He outwitted Slimy at every trick and turn through application to the job and sheer hard work, but in the end he was unceremoniously dumped.

There was no happy ending in this case even though James stuck it to the bitter end. He just had no idea at the time that his Slimy Frog would use him the way he did. However, James emerged from this fracas, which lasted for several months, a much wiser and stronger individual, with an even stronger belief in himself because he had survived and not been cowed. After this performance and the destructiveness of the attack by Slimy, James could have gone in one of two directions. The first direction might have been a complete retreat that could have been the beginning of the end of him. He could have become a Fantasizer or a Visualiser or both, and justifiably so. He could have dropped out of circulation and lost any sense of ambition.

Fortunately, James chose the remaining path, which was to conduct a thorough post mortem on his time with Slimy Frog. He wrote everything down and in as much detail as possible with a list of things he knew he had done correctly and another list of situations where, by his own admission, he may have faltered. The only problem on his second list was his inability to 'gel' with Slimy. Somewhere the chemistry was lacking but James could not pinpoint it. In the end, this became a non-issue because in answering the questions 'where did he go wrong?' (nowhere) and 'what did he do right?' (everything), they became the most important answers for him. He also tried to ascertain why he was having so much difficulty winning over Slimy – there was no 'chemistry' between the two of them and the Frog made no attempt to find any. To the final question of what he would do differently next time, his reply was nothing because there was not going to be a next time with this particular Frog. Having satisfied himself through his analysis that the problem belonged to Slimy, James no longer concerned himself with it and turned his attention to other possibilities.

Morgan was also duped into working with the same Slimy individual on a similar project and was initially accorded the same kind of treatment. However, for some strange reason, Slimy began to react positively towards Morgan's presence, although basically Morgan's attitude was no different from James' attitude. Morgan subsequently emerged from the experience with Slimy as his friend and the Frog went on to become a mentor to Morgan in his quest for success.

Why James could not make the grade we will never know. It was a matter of chemistry and that is why we advocate that if you have strong doubts about cultivating a relationship with your Slimy Frog, sometimes discretion is the better part of valour. James actually mapped out a slightly different plan for his advancement with different people and is now doing exceptionally well.

To conclude this chapter, let's look at another Slimy Frog outcome that was a bit different from the two above and a novel solution to the problem.

Vera was a hard working purchasing manager in a large company. She was good at her work, had inexhaustible patience and was definitely a 'people person' having had plenty of practice in working with Lesser Frogs and one of two of the Slimy variety. One particular afternoon she had scheduled an appointment to see the representative of a company who had blotted their copybook in the past with Vera's company. The representative who arrived in Vera's office was the managing director, no less, of this particular company. The MD was smart, autocratic and dictatorial, more or less demanding that Vera purchase her company's products. Vera listened patiently to all the MD's demands, but in the end decided that she would think for a little while longer before making any purchase. The MD was therefore not amused when Vera politely declined, and she left in a huff! Vera was heartily glad to see her go and hoped that this particular individual would not pester her again. Even though her company had a previous problem with the MD's company, Vera could see some advantages of doing business with them, but she needed time to think. Approximately three months later, Vera went on a trip to the blotted copybook Company's headquarters and was relieved to find that she would be dealing with the MD of a different division. You can imagine her shock when she arrived at the headquarters to find not only the new host to greet her, but also, hovering in the background, the Slimy Frog MD of three months previously! Vera was mortified. She was quite used to dealing with and winning over difficult people, but this MD was a challenge she didn't particularly relish. Vera very quickly gave some thought to a strategy and came up with a novel idea. She decided that the best way of dealing with this Slimy Frog was to ignore her completely, since she was not her official host. The autocratic MD did not like this one little bit, but her hands were tied, as she was not the host on this occasion. By the end of her visit, Vera thereby successfully reversed the situation that previously existed when she was in the company of the autocratic MD, by making the Slimy Frog adapt to her framework because she had no choice. That was the start of a much better relationship between the two women.

Even if you decide at any point that a relationship between you and Slimy Frog is not to be, then take time to remind yourself that you are a very valuable person with lots of talent and knowledge to share. Sooner, rather than later, you will find the person who is going to recognise and share these ideals with you and further your career.

10

Courting the Slimy Frog

The aristocracy went a-courting ...

The English language has developed wonderful words to describe the nature of two loving individuals coming together in that process prior to the snog, or whatever else it might lead to. The aristocracy went a-courting whilst the middle classes were wooing or spooning, the working classes were walking out together or at the most base end, were sniffing round the honey pot. Whatever phrases were used for the journey, all roads led in the same direction to the land of consummation.

It is just so within the business world and the snogging process is just as necessary. Whatever word we use to describe that process and whatever the road we take, they all lead to the consummation of the deal and the completion of the project. In everyday courting, the suitor seeks to please his intended mate by making her receptive to seduction. Likewise in business courting, the suitor is seeking to create a feeling of receptivity and seduction in order to gain something from the Frog.

The amorous suitor will spend much time and put great effort into getting to know his love. He is concerned about what it is she would like and as his knowledge grows, his gifts become more appropriate, the flowers are the right blooms and the chocolates the correct variety, the excursion is to the right place and the meals are in the most favoured restaurants. It is this process of tuning in to the mate that draws the couple together. The closer they become, the easier the communication. It is the ease of communication, both verbal and physical that leads to intimacy. It is the intimacy that is the substance of the relationship.

For those couples involved in the natural process of a chance meeting followed by the mutual grooming and provision of mutual pleasure, the process is fun, natural and mutually agreeable. If, however, the couple are brought together by arrangement, perhaps by well-meaning parents, the process may only work with luck and much effort, though for some it does not work at all.

There is nothing natural in the arranged relationship. The relationship does not simply happen and it doesn't grow. It has to be built as two strangers struggle to first discover each other and then attempt to make the situation work, as in the case of the Slimy Frog. Not all relationships work – some will always fail whether they are natural or arranged.

It is the same in business. There will be the natural relationship where your eyes meet those of the Frog across a crowded pond and the natural process of courting will begin and hopefully lead to snogging. Sometimes, the relationship will be arranged, such as in the case of Slimy or Lesser Frogs. You will have to work to find common ground and discover the nature of your Frog before successful courting can commence.

In the drive to find a mate, it is common today to place an advert in a lonely-hearts type column either in a newspaper or on the Internet. When doing this, individuals have to describe what it is they are offering and describe what it is they are looking for. So there are adverts such as 'Batman seeks girl wonder' or 'fun, fat and forty seeks partner for ...' In all these cases the individuals have put some thought into how they see themselves, how it is they would like others to see themselves and what it is they are looking for in another person.

The business world is exactly the same. What do you have to offer and what are you looking for or, what are you selling and what are you buying? It is important to have a clear shopping list. When you go to the shop and you want to buy a packet of crackers, you do not go into a shop and ask for a loaf of bread. You know what you want before you get there. If you go out without a shopping list you might end up with a loaf of bread and a packet of crackers leaving one to go stale on the cupboard shelf, wasting resources. Decide what sort of Frog you want and be clear about what it is you want from him before you go shopping, using the method described in 'Who to Snog'.

Unless a natural meeting occurs, selecting a Frog is like selecting a partner and involves being clear about what it is you want. Having read the chapters on Personality Types and Dealing with Bad Breath, you should at least have some idea of what is not acceptable to you. Keep this in mind, as it is now time to give some thought to action and long-term strategic planning – not to be confused with 'Strategies' in Chapter 5. So in this chapter, as well as suggestions for action, it is also a checklist of those resources needed for the snog, together with some reminders about your personal safety.

Understanding the framework of the Slimy Frog

We hope that through reading this Frog snoggers guide so far you are more able to understand something about the inner workings of both yourself and your potential or actual Frog. Each of us exists in a personal framework that dictates how we live and what we do. These frameworks reflect the structure of our personality through the operation of our self-concept, our access to our emotions and our ability to act. For most people, their attitudes, and therefore the frameworks in which they live, are fixed. It is only when individuals wake up psychologically that they realise they are able to effect change in their lives. Most people only change because they have no choice – usually at the point of pain. The person who is psychologically awake changes if, and when, he or she desires it. All change takes energy and it is only when we are aware of the need to change that we can plan and assess what we will need to make the change happen.

Up to the point of consciousness, people remain blissfully unaware of the differences between themselves and others. Before waking has occurred, most people live in the belief that all other 'normal people', whatever normal is, feel and think in the same way that they do – and this is not true. Because of this mistaken assumption most people fail to communicate and become ineffective in their attempts to achieve their aims. Such failure leads to a common sense of dissatisfaction and a negative self-image.

Are you clear about yourself and the framework you live in? Your framework is the structure you have created around you to express the way you see yourself. This includes your hairstyle, spectacles, clothes, car, house and friends – everything that is you. If you look at those you feel comfortable with, they will have similar frameworks and you will find that you will like similar things. Is your framework fixed? Are your attitudes fixed? The more adaptable your framework, the greater will be the range of your friends. If you find you have two different groups of friends that you get on well with but you know that the two groups would not get on well with one another your framework is adaptable to two sides. The more different types of people you are able to feel comfortable with the more flexible your framework.

When your framework is fully functioning and adaptable, you will feel comfortable and not threatened, interacting with any of the personality types we have examined – physical, social, intellectual, emotional, mental, intuitive, and creative. Even if they have bad breath or are real toads, you will be able to match them and talk their language.

Check your framework

Look around you at your home, office, car, clothes and so on. How do you think other people will experience you? I have an experience with cars. I don't really like them and yet I manage to clock around forty thousand miles each year. For me a car is a metal box that has a wheel at each corner and one that you hold in your hands. As long as it continues to start and stop and keep me warm, it is doing its job. My only demand is a decent radio cassette and a compact disc player. Out of choice, I would keep a car until it dropped and then bury it in the scrap pile.

Because in my business I am a snogger, I need to attend wall-to-wall meetings, to set up business. Over the years, I became aware that the courting process was starting in the car park. I would roll up in my old Hyundai banger and park it along side the gleaming new BMWs, Jags, Mercs and the occasional Roller. I found that in the snobbery of the Frog Snogger's clubs, I was not cutting the mustard and was being derided because I was seen to be unsuccessful with wheels that were too old and tatty. The first time I was aware of this was when I had just put a deal together with the Managing Director of a train company. We stood in the boardroom, both pin-striped, and shook hands with the firm and confident grip of those who had struck a bargain. Together we walked out of the building chatting about families, leather brief cases swinging. He strolled over to his top-of-the-range Rover, flourishing his electronic key which created a clunk as the central locking mechanism unlocked all the doors. I saw the look on his face when I went over to one of my favourite old bangers and struggled to get the key into the well-worn lock.

At that moment his attitude to me changed I could see the look of disdain on his face. In the boardroom, we were on a level playing field, working as equals. In the car park, the mismatch of our frameworks put future negotiations at risk. After several such incidents, I have given in and I have adapted my framework to be more acceptable to my Frogs. I now buy new cars and change them every two to three years. The same is true for all facets of our framework – we need to develop, grow and adapt to fit our framework to whatever situation we are in. When we are skilled, we are able to adjust our framework to the appropriate face to improve our communication and courting.

Use the exercises below to check out the condition of your framework. Ask yourself how do others see you? Whilst doing this, think of Frogs you have tried to snog or are snogging. Is there a match or mismatch of frameworks between you both? Matching your framework to that of the Frog is the basic tool of courting because then they will accept you and allow intimacy to develop.

Your Framework

To see ourselves as others see us

Your Physical framework
Look at the physical side of your framework.
How will others experience you physically?
If your physical framework is strong, you will find physical interactions easy. You play blow for blow in physical banter and game play. You are sporty, watch sport or use a gym or take some form of exercise. If someone asks you what you thought about the match last night or asks you which team you supported, you know what they are talking about. You find yourself at ease in the company of physical types. When someone crosses you, you would like to hit him or her. On a scale of 1 to 12, how strong is your physical framework?

Score your physical framework and consider that if you were snogging a physical Frog, how good would be the match? Would you need to make an effort to adapt your framework to fit in with a physical Frog? If so, how would you do this?

Your Social Framework

Now look at your social framework.

How will others experience you socially?

If your social framework is strong, will you find it comfortable to be with people that are new to you. You find it easy to get to know people or Frogs and to know about them. You enjoy talking socially and you are able to make small talk. You are able to fit in, keep your mouth shut and avoid conflict. You can also be a bit nosy, like a good time and enjoy a bit of gossip.

Score your social framework. If you were snogging a social Frog, do your frameworks match? Would you need to make an effort to adapt your framework to fit in with a social Frog? How would you do this?

Your Intellectual Framework

What about you intellectual framework?

How will others experience your adaptability?

If your intellectual framework is strong, you are a list writer and even make lists of lists. You enjoy change and new experience and you become easily bored. You are enthusiastic about new and novel ideas. You are quick witted and able to respond quickly in an argument but you have problems making decisions. You are a procrastinator and when you get bored you have problems seeing things through to completion.

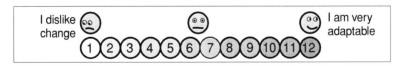

Score your intellectual framework in comparison to that of your intellectual Frog. Would you need to make an effort to adapt your framework to fit in with an intellectual Frog? How would you do this?

135

Your Emotional Framework

Now let us look at your emotional framework.

How will others experience your need for recognition?

If your emotional framework is strong, you feel things deeply and you seek recognition from others. You enjoy having and using power and you are concerned about how others experience you, but will deny this. You react badly to personal criticism and hold grudges for a long time.

Does your emotional framework score fit with that of your emotional Frog? Would you need to make an effort to adapt your framework to fit in with an emotional Frog? How would you do this?

Your Mental Framework

Consider your mental framework.

How will others experience your organisational abilities which are indicative of your mental framework?

If your mental framework is strong, you will be tidy and organised. You always arrive on time and hate to be late. Your memory will be fairly good. You like those around you to be rational and you feel uncomfortable with shows of emotion. Since you are rather fixed in your ideas and opinions, you will not feel comfortable with change.

Score your mental framework and consider if you are snogging a mental Frog how much might you match? Would you need to make any adaptations to fit with a mental Frog? If so, how would you do this?

Your Intuitive Framework

Look at your intuitive framework.

How will others experience your sensitivity that belongs to your intuitive framework?

If your intuitive framework is strong, you will be able to tune into the feelings of others and you will be sensitive to the needs of others. You will strive to live in an atmosphere of peace and harmony and will have strong feelings about right and wrong. You will have problems acting in negative ways outside your belief system and will sometimes look down on others as being shallow or leading meaningless lives. You might feel you are superior.

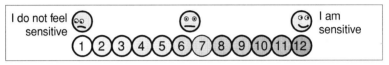

Consider if you were snogging an intuitive Frog how much might you match your frameworks? Would you need to adapt your framework to fit in with an intuitive Frog and if so, how would you do this?

Your Creative Framework

How will others experience your ability to solve problems within your creative framework?

If your creative framework is strong, you will be intrigued by problems and seek solutions as well as coming up with original ideas. You will be able to inspire others into action and others may expect you to inspire them into action. You may have a conflict in that you are able to inspire others to act positively or negatively.

Score your creative framework and consider if you had a creative Frog, how much might you match? Would you need to make an effort to adapt your framework to fit in with a creative Frog? How would you do this?

Your Fantasy Framework

Finally, let us look at your fantasy framework.

How will others experience your ability to dream?

If your fantasy framework is strong, you enjoy daydreaming and you will have unrealistic ideas. You will have an unrealistic faith in the sincerity of others. You will always avoid conflict. After events have taken place you will re-write the script and change the story line to a more acceptable one. You find it easier to deal with animals than people. You will not want others to tell you the truth or make you face reality. When your bubble is burst you are deeply hurt and want to get away from people.

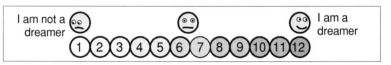

If your Frog were a dreamy Frog how would your frameworks match? If you needed to make an effort to adapt your framework to fit in with a dreamy Frog, how would you do this?

Flirting

Flirting is part of the courting process that is mutual and unseen. Flirting can only take place when both you and the Frog are talking the same language. When your framework and the framework of the Frog are the same or similar, you will be talking the same language and be able to communicate successfully.

When your frameworks do not match, your behaviour will be seen as inappropriate, wrong, awkward, stupid, offensive and/or, insensitive. In short, you will not be communicating successfully. Courting is a process of seduction. Seduction requires sensitive and appropriate actions and responses.

Boundaries

When courting a Frog, you may have to modify your framework and assume an identity that you are not comfortable with. You will be outside your usual framework away from your comfort zone, playing away from home, speaking a foreign language and attempting to understand another currency, which has been discussed on an individual basis in Chapter 8 – Dealing with Bad Breath.

It is important that you set your boundaries and that you are clear about just how far it is you are prepared to go to get what you want. There is an important issue here about personal safety. If, for example, you are snogging an insensitive, physical or emotional, power-hungry Frog it is as well that others know where you are. Make sure you have a way of contacting people if necessary.

The problems of personal vulnerability are mainly to do with female snoggers snogging insensitive males – but not always. I know of many examples of people who had started out attempting to achieve their goal and were taken advantage of on the way – so there is a need to be alert at all times.

There was once a middle-aged woman who, when young, decided it was worth it to have sex with an older, power-hungry Frog to get what she wanted. She did not enjoy the experience and the old Frog later became her father-in-law. The Frog's son, her husband, knew nothing about the situation. The Frog used blackmail to continue the sexual relationship after the marriage, which carried on until the Frog died. The relationship lasted over 25 years. She described herself as having been raped twice a week throughout her married life, even when she was pregnant.

The positive process

Beyond all such negativity, mutual snogging when both parties are using the same framework can be exhilarating, fulfilling and a lot of fun. The important issue is that the relationship is mutual. When you are out there taking from Frogs, what is it that you have to give in return? If you can give to Frogs, especially Slimy Frogs, they will be more compliant and it will be easier to get what you want. When designing your courting strategy make sure you understand, to the best of your ability, the personality and framework of your Frog and do what you can, using that knowledge, to put them at ease by adapting your framework to theirs. If they see you as one of 'them', life is so much easier.

A case in point, socially, but it could easily apply to the business world, is about a couple, John and Natalie, who moved into a new flat. They had met the couple in the flat below and had already experienced resentment towards them from the husband, Bernard. The Slimy Frog status was confirmed because Bernard refused to move his car when John and Natalie were moving in. Natalie, sensing the antagonism, kept out of the way, so it became a conflict between two men, both with physical frameworks but totally incompatible.

John recognised what the problem was, and decided that he was going to have to adjust his framework in order to become friendly with this Slimy Frog, Bernard. John recognised the problem but he knew that Bernard did not and furthermore Bernard would never be able to realise that there was incompatibility. Since they were to be neighbours, and since John felt that it was better that they be good neighbours, he had to adjust him framework to accommodate Bernard.

After their initial confrontation, John became conciliatory towards Bernard and started to mend fences, even though Bernard was the one who put up the fences in the first place. Gradually John wore down Bernard who started to relax a little, but still a final hurdle remained. Natalie hit on the brilliant idea of getting John to ask Bernard for some advice about an electric problem. This was the turning point where frameworks met and things started to improve. The thaw set in rapidly because Bernard felt that he had been courted and that he was needed. Since then, the two couples have been the best of friends.

11

Dealing with Toads

*When you shake hands with a toad,
count your fingers afterwards*

Coping with being double-crossed

Have you ever met a Toad? Do you know what a Toad looks like?
There is a difference between Frogs and Toads. Toads are another
species altogether although Toads are often mistaken for Frogs
because they look so much alike. Toads sometimes pose as Frogs and
fool the odd passing snogger on their way to progress their pet

project. The difference between a Frog and a Toad is profound. Frogs are essentially useful – Toads are not. A Frog will, in the end, help you and may even become your friend. Toads do not help you and they are certainly not made of 'friend' material.

When you shake hands with a Toad, count your fingers afterwards to make sure he hasn't kept one for later. Frogs may be slimy, they may smell a bit and even have bad breath, but they are not Toads.

In the main, with the right treatment, the Frog will play his part in your scheme but the Toad will not.

The problem with the average Toad is that as well as being very hard to spot, he has never been educated in the school of fair play, moral codes and ethical behaviour and worst of all, he does not play by the Frog-snogging rules. It is sad but true that in most cases you only discover that what you thought was a Frog is actually a Toad when you find he has gone back on his word. Despite your best snogging, he has not done what it is he promised he would do for you. Maybe he has done the opposite and completely messed up your plans. He may have had you dangling on a piece of string and was simply using you to get what he wanted from you, without giving anything in return.

In the worst extreme, he will commit the ultimate sin and steal your idea, product or project and used it for himself or to his own advantage. The Toad may be a thief and should never be trusted. Commonly, when a Toad has finished with you, he will cast you aside like a spent match. You are no longer any use to him. You are a depleted resource and you have become history like yesterday's news. You are left feeling violated, used and abused.

When you have been Toaded, you may well feel in need some rest and recuperation – or even psychotherapy. When you have been Toaded you will feel mixtures of emotion and anger. Toading can wreck your self-confidence and your sense of self-esteem. After Toading you will often feel like the victim of a hit and run, left bruised and battered in the road. In your case, the emergency services will not be called and it will be up to you to drag yourself to your feet and get on with life.

Coming to terms with being Toaded is like coming to terms with bereavement. First there is the disbelief. Next comes the grief followed closely by the emotion. Behind this, come feelings of violence crossed with feelings of impotence. Murder may be in your mind and the violent feelings may be in your heart. These negative feelings will need to be expressed and resolved. In some cases you might decide to retaliate in an attempt to get even. Beware of becoming a Toad yourself. Many good souls have become Toads because they themselves were Toaded in the first place. Sometimes justice has to be meted out by a higher court.

There is a phrase used in the Northwest of England, though I have heard variations in other places and other countries, that often comes to mind at these times which is, 'what goes around comes around'. This is the equivalent of the eastern idea of karma, the law of cause and effect that is described in Bible through the parable of the sower which suggests the idea that as we sow so shall we reap. To put it simply, 'everyone gets theirs' in the end.

When we have been wronged, many of us want the perpetrator to suffer as we have suffered, to feel the same pain. We want to hurt them as they have hurt us. It might be useful to consider what effect these feelings have on us.

When you are filled with so much anger and a passionate desire for revenge, when you lie awake at night planning the worst things you can create in the darkest recesses of your imagination, when your heart is racing with the adrenalin coursing through your veins as you clench your fists and grit your teeth; when you push away the dinner plate because your stomach is in a turmoil to the extent that you are unable to eat and sometimes you are even sick with anxious tension; when you are so up-tight that the slightest thing leads you to let rip your short-fused anger on those around you; it is you, your body and your relationships that you are damaging – not your Toad.

- When the Toad is sitting somewhere relaxing in a metaphorical sun, at his ease, it is your system which is suffering from lack of sleep and anxious images of revenge.

- When the Toad is working out at the gym, it is your arteries that are hardening from too much unused adrenalin flooding your system in your state of anxiety.

- When the Toad is out enjoying a meal in his favourite restaurant, it is your stomach that is heading for ulceration due to hyper-production of acid and lack of appetite.

- When the Toad goes home in the evening and enjoys being in the warm bosom of his family, it is your family relationships that are bearing the brunt of your frustration and thwarted ambition.

When you have been Toaded, you can generate enough negative energy to light a small town for a month. If you were able to turn this massive storehouse of negative energy into positive energy by promoting your next project and not wasting it in useless and unrealisable fantasies of revenge, what a powerful Frog snogger you would become.

My word is my bond – verbal agreements mean nothing to a Toad.

The Baltic Exchange in London deals with shipping and cargoes from all over the world. The Exchange has worked for many hundreds of years on the basis of contracts and agreements being a matter of verbal confirmation, in other words – 'my word is my bond'. Many millions of pounds worth of shipping, in the form of future crops of coffee, tea, sugar and so on, are traded with a nod and a wink in the certain knowledge that both parties will stand by the agreement. There are some aspects of contract law that recognise a verbal agreement as a legally binding contract but these may be difficult and expensive to enforce and require some sort of proof, usually in the form of an independent witness. It is easy to fall into partnership-type relationships on the basis of mutual trust.

Many business and personal relationships founder because the basic issues of the agreement were never formalised. It is most important to know in advance what will happen to the business and, as it progresses, how the assets should be divided at the point of separation. Even if you have made a verbal agreement that you feel happy with, you have no way of knowing that the other party has the same understanding as you. It is important when snogging to be aware of the risks you are in involving yourself in when undertaking the snog.

- What are the limits of your liability?
- Does the current situation leave you vulnerable if the agreement comes to an end or fails prematurely?
- Ask yourself if you need a written contract in the relationship with this particular Frog.

Often the suggestion of a contract, or the idea of a written agreement, is not raised for fear of offending the Frog or scaring him away before we get what we want. The Frog is of little use if, in the end, we lose everything for fear of getting an agreement in the first place.

A genuine Frog would expect you to cover your self both legally and professionally. A genuine Frog has nothing to hide. So just how do you know the Frog you can trust? Trust is an interesting concept.

One of our mentors suggested that 'trust' is what happens to a chicken before it goes into the oven! It is tied up and unable to move. It can be like that when we trust Frogs to do what it is they say they will do. We can become tied up in expectant anticipation waiting for this trusted Frog to perform. But with a written agreement, we can loose these bonds because we have ways of enforcing the contract, or getting out of the situation if we so wish. If we are not careful, we allow ourselves to become fixed in a situation where we lose the flexibility and agility to react to the circumstances of the moment.

The Ten Rules of Making Agreements and Working Successfully with Toads

There are ten basic rules you should follow when setting up a working relationship with someone else.

Rule One: Just because someone says something, it does not mean that it is so. Toads lie.

Sadly there are few people who can stick by their word being their bond. To them, the truth is a moveable feast and they assume that they can re-write history to meet current needs. Just because someone says something, it does not follow that it is necessarily so. Just because someone says they will do something for you, it does not follow that they will. Belief in what people tell us is like trust. If this belief is misplaced, you may find yourself fixed in a position where you are unable to respond to another opportunity because you are waiting for a Toad you thought was a Frog, to perform. Indeed, can your word be your bond? There is always the chance that a better deal may come up and temptation can be a powerful thing. At least, when an agreement or contract has been formally drawn up and signed, you know that both parties are tied to it.

Rule Two: Get your agreement in writing. Toads go back on their word.

Always get it in writing. The written word is the main form of evidence that is used when attempting to enforce a contract or agreement, but make sure that the wording is correct and makes sense or it will remain unenforceable. It is not always necessary to involve a solicitor in preparing the wording but at the least you should check the context of your words with others to ensure that someone reading it understands what you mean and that there are no loopholes.

Rule Three: Have a witness. Toads will deny it ever took place.

When signing something, ensure someone you can trust witnesses it. If possible, make it someone that you would be able to call upon as a witness in a court of law or a mediation hearing. You need someone who is able to be your witness in fact as well as on paper. The same is true for the verbal agreement. If it is witnessed and can be shown beyond reasonable doubt to have taken place you can enforce an implied or actual contract.

Rule Four: Always confirm verbal agreements in writing. Toads deny that conversations ever took place.

This is useful when you have a witness and is vital if you do not. Factual confirmation that a conversation took place or an agreement was made will strengthen your case in later proceedings. Write a letter or a memo to the Toad. Whenever possible send a copy to a relevant third party. In this way, others have noted the agreement of the Toad.

The third party might be another colleague or a Frogs involved in the project, a bank manager, an accountant, or in the case of an organisation, the Toad's boss or superior. When you write, make simple statements such as:

'Dear Toad. I am writing to confirm that when I met you in the car park today, you said *this* and we both agreed *that*, and that you undertook to do the *business* at an agreed price of *xyz*.'

Always end such communications with a qualifying statement such as; 'if for any reason this account does not match with your experience,' or, 'if you require further clarification, please do not hesitate to contact me'. In any event, you need a statement that is saying to the Toad 'if you do not agree with what I am saying you had better tell me or I will hold you to this agreement because you have accepted it by default'.

In some situations, you might need to be more direct, 'please confirm that you agree with this version of events'. You might even ask for confirmation by a certain time or date. Remember to remain vigilant. The pond has murky depths and the Toad will pull you down to the bottom.

Rule Five: Be careful where you sign. Toads play cunning tricks.

This may sound a melodramatic but it is within the experience of the authors that it is possible for a Toad to leave a gap between the end of the last typed clause and the space for your signature and his signature. This gap will be large enough to add one or more clauses that you did not know about or agree to, after you have signed the agreement. If there is a gap between the last paragraph and where you are signing draw several lines through this space, or put your initials at the end of the last word.

Rule Six: Read the small print. Toads have good eyesight.

Most people sign a myriad documents without reading them. The Devil is in the small print. You only need to claim on a house insurance policy after a house break in, or a personal health policy after an illness to discover that there is always a 'because' which means that the company is unable to pay. It was there all the time in the small print – you just didn't read the small print.

Rule Seven: Never assume anything. Toads hope that you will.

Whatever your form of agreement, implied agreement or contract, never make any assumptions. Clarify everything you possibly can. Sit down on your own, or with a close associate and go through every permutation of events that you can imagine. Check out everything, cross the t's and dot the i's. Never assume that you know what is meant – ask and, if you are not happy with the explanation, ask again and again until you are happy. Never assume others will make arrangements, pay bills, do jobs and so on – check it and then double-check it.

Rule Eight: 'Without prejudice'. Even when you prejudicial about the actions of a Toad.

When writing something that you do not want held against you in a court of law, the phrase 'without prejudice' gives you the best chance of a get-out clause. The phrase means that you are not making any presumptions in this case and that what you are stating is the way it appears to you. It gives the other party a chance to respond prior to legal action. The phrase also implies that legal action will be following which can be a powerful communication in its own right. This is not a 100% safety net. The laws of libel still apply. If in doubt always take legal advice.

Rule Nine: Cover yourself when you leave things out of an agreement. The Toad will not let you put them in later.

It is easy to forget something especially when you are feeling pressured and in the middle of making a deal. If you do make a genuine error a friend or a well-snogged Frog will point it out to you – a Toad will not. Your error may be the very thing that allows the Toad to cheat you. When writing quotes, reports, proposals, recommendations and even invoices always add the phrase 'Excepting Errors and Omissions', often abbreviated to E E&O. This phrase really means 'plus anything else I have forgotten to include in the document at this time, or that I might want to include at a later date'. It allows you to have draft one, draft two and so on. On invoices the phrase allows you to go back and get missed payments. It allows for extra work done that was not recognised or realised at the time of invoicing. Reclaims can then be sorted out even after a contract has come to a close.

Rule Ten: Always keeps a copy of your agreement or contract safe. The Toad will.

An agreement may be only one single sheet of paper. If you end up going to law, that single sheet of paper may be all that you have to support your claim. Agreements also grow in value. Successful projects increase in value, as does the value of any contract that might also have a sale value. Keep all copies of contracts securely and if you can, keep them in a safe. You might make several copies of your agreement so that in the event of theft or fire, you still have at least one copy to work on. Never put it past a Toad to steal agreements. Keep them safe.

There are your ten rules for making agreements and working successfully with a Toad. Follow them, and he will never get the better of you, no matter how hard he tries.

Broken agreements

In the authors' experience, most cases of broken agreements come about because people fail to get the right agreement in the first place. Either the agreement was unrealistic or we failed to make it workable or, at best, we failed to recognise a Toad because we thought he was a Frog. This is not a blame issue. There is no blame unless we make it so. When things go wrong, we do not beat ourselves, or each other, over it. We attempt to use each crisis as a learning experience. It sounds a bit of a contradiction, but very often problems create opportunities. We may not like some experiences and we certainly do not enjoy being Toaded, but in the main, we can laugh and start again. Next time the sky opens and the big finger points at you, it is not because you have just won the lottery but because it is your turn to grow, to take the chance and use what you learn to become a better snogger.

Do It Yourself

One lesson we learned very early on was after some song scripts were lifted and presented as other people's work. In fact, the annals are littered with cases where others have stolen original ideas and written material. It is a wise idea, initially, before you get legal advice, to establish dated ownership of your ideas, projects, writings, electronic media and so on. Place the original valuable commodity in a sealed package, so that the seals can be seen to be intact. Take the package to the post office and mail it to yourself as a registered delivery. When you receive it do not open it, keep it. You now have a sealed, dated version of whatever you wanted to confirm as an original piece of work. If you are put in the position where you have to prove ownership, you have an example that can be taken into Court and opened there in front of witnesses – a secure idea, and all for the small cost of a stamp.

149

Late payments

Late payments are a nightmare, especially when cash-flow is tight. Late payment or non-payment can lead to bankruptcy for the sole trader or the small business. You have to decide how much time you are prepared to let the customer have before payment. This is normally incorporated in getting the trading terms and conditions right in the first place. The authors have a rule whereby late payment or non-payment leads to the issuing of a County Court summons. This action is drastic and almost always leads to business from that customer drying up completely. Local Councils and Health Authorities in Britain are renowned for being bad payers. One Health Authority would commonly pay three months in arrears on an agreement of thirty days net. When this ran to six months, and all the usual statements and 'it would be nice if you paid this bill' letters had failed, the only option was the threat to issue a County Court summons. In this case the bill was paid in full within seven days but we never worked for that health authority again, by their choice not ours. In the end, who wants to work for a bad payer?

Bad debts

I have had bad debts. People who do not pay leave me with a sense of outrage. In most cases, this leads me to raise a County Court action to reclaim the debt. My principle is that no debt is too small to be collected, even if the cost of collecting it is really greater than the debt itself, but we all have to make a stand somewhere. When a multi-millionaire, who had just sold his house for £3.5 million, did not pay me the £25 he owed me, I was happy to spend the £35 it cost to raise the County Court papers. I got my money. People who do not pay after commissioning work are Toads.

I have another case in point. It is 5.50 am on May 14, 2000. I have been lying awake for a while, partly because my wife Marie is restless, being heavily pregnant with Joshua, our third child, my fourth son, who is due in four weeks, and partly from the fact that I have been Toaded and have not acted as I would normally. Tossing it around in my head, and considering that I am writing this book giving you advice on dealing with Toads, it seems that I should put my money where my mouth is and do something about it. The story goes something like this.

In November 1999 I did some work for an international company and have not as yet received payment. I have been Toaded. It all happened when Marie, who is a dietician working in the British National Health Service, was being headhunted by a major pharmaceutical company. There was a lot of snogging going on. Marie does freelance work for a particular representative of the company – let us call the representative Sylvia. The company put on road shows for doctors and nurses and used other health professionals and experts to present programmes on various topics, while Sylvia did the soft sell for the drug company in the background. Sylvia, who as a true and dedicated rep, would snog anyone anyhow, anytime and anywhere if there was a chance to make a percentage, had brought Marie to the notice of her boss. I suspect that Sylvia would have been on a percentage if she landed Marie for the company. So we had a line of snogging setting up. The boss was snogging Sylvia and Sylvia was snogging Marie.

To increase her chances of making her kill, Sylvia started snogging me and gave me well-paid presentations and lectures in the road shows. Her snogging technique was mainly to take me on one side while Marie was doing her bit in the show and snog me in the hope that I would snog Marie for her. The odds increased as Marie and I got invited to banquets and were being snogged by Sylvia, her boss and the entire team. Then the boss took Marie out to lunch and snogged her directly with offers of riches and reward. Generally then, there was a great deal of snogging and chapped lips all round.

Marie could not decide what she should do. Then she became pregnant. At this point, Marie ceased to be a snoggable commodity for Sylvia because there was no percentage. The snogging stopped overnight. Sylvia disappeared into the background and my last invoice is still not paid. This is a small fee of £150.00 plus the good old VAT. Sylvia turned out to be not the Frog we took her for but a Toad and I had been Toaded. Now this left me with a dilemma. It is possible that Marie might want to work with the company in the future and also Marie and Sylvia have a sort of friendship. Sylvia and her partner did came to the 'knees-up' after our wedding, but that was when she was snogging and playing the part of Frog. No sign of being a Toad at that time. To date, I have sent Sylvia several statements attempting to get payment without being heavy because I felt that I should not rock the boat between her and Marie or between Marie and the company.

Marie did ring her and she did promise to pay, but no cheque has popped through the letterbox so far. There is a strong lesson here about mixing business with pleasure but Frogs can so easily become friends before they turn out to be Toads. That can be dangerous. So it is beginning to look as though the matter will have to go to court. The next question is how do I do that?

Going to law

Going to Court is always a risky business. You might lose. The British press abounds with stories of those who have taken people to court to claim damages for libellous statements and lost, often at a cost of several million pounds. In the County Court System, access to court procedure is limited by the amount of the claim and as this varies, you will need to check it at the time. Assuming your case falls within the remit of the County Court, the fee for taking the action plus enforcement costs of any successful outcome is all you pay. For me the most important point of taking a County Court action is that the individual or company is entered on the list of bad payers for seven years – the list used by credit companies who will turn down future application for credit on the part of the Toad. This process has three functions for me.

- ☑ It makes me feel better and I cease to be a victim.
- ☑ It limits the ability of the Toad to damage others.
- ☑ It makes life difficult for the Toad in such a way that he might just learn something.

So back to the plot – what about Sylvia and my fee?

It would seem at this stage there is nothing left to do but to raise the County Court Writ. So I need to write to her again stating my intention of doing just this. It is normal in these cases to make the statement that if payment is not received by a certain date then legal proceedings will follow. My next decision is whether I should take the writ out against her or the company. As a budget holder, she paid cheques directly to me in the past. So it would seem that the best strategy is to write to her directly threatening a writ against her and sending a copy to the company. This would seem to give me the best chance of getting my money back because I suspect the company will put pressure on Sylvia to clear the debt. They do after all have a name to maintain. To make sure the point goes home I will send a copy to her, one to her boss, and one to the managing director.

Next I need to decide what it is I will claim for in the court. If the Toad pays after the letter threatening legal action I cannot claim my additional costs, but if she ignores my letter the structure of my claim will be something like:

The original fee	150.00
The VAT already paid	26.00
Approximate interest on the fee since the due date	5.00
Approximate interest on the VAT already paid	.76
Costs of raising statements 4 x £10.00	40.00
My cost involved in chasing the money.	
3 hours at £10.00	30.00
The court fee for raising the writ	50.00
Total claimed	301.76

So when I have finished this chapter, I will write the letter to Sylvia, with a copy to her boss and one to the managing director giving them twenty one days to pay my invoice of £150.00 plus VAT or I will take a writ claiming £307.76.

I am just now making final corrections to this manuscript, several weeks later, and I can happily report that the cheque arrived in the morning post. In the end, I wrote to the company, copy to the MD. Payment took ten days from the letter. I have not seen Sylvia yet, though I suspect that there will not be any more work from that quarter.

To complete the story, Joshua was born at my own fair hand on July 8th, and continues to thrive. At six weeks, when he could focus his eyes, I noticed how much he manipulates those around him by smiling to obtain the oohs and aahs. I think that babies are really embryo frog snoggers.

Mediation

When agreements are broken or fees not paid, there is the other option of mediation. Professional mediators do exist. Solicitors and counsellors may run some mediation services. Professional mediators, although less expensive than full representation in a court of law, are not cheap and the arrangement for meeting the costs should be agreed before mediation starts. In reality, a mediator can be anyone respected by both parties, on the basis that both parties agree to abide by whatever the decision the mediator might come to.

Know your Toad

When you discover that your Frog is actually a Toad, attempt to read him. The Toad, like you and I, lives in a world of wants, needs and securities. Refer back to our personality archetypes and identify your Toad. Check Chapter Eight on Dealing with Bad Breath. Develop a strategy. Most important of all remember that Toads, like bullies, come in two major types and it is important to know the difference. There are those that will back down and give up when challenged, and those that have a psychopathic tendency to act without conscience or take into account the feelings of others.

Beware! Psychopaths can be dangerous.

12

Where do we go from here?

"You can't make an omelette without breaking eggs."
(Maggie Thatcher)

Or to put it another way:

You can't have a good snog without opening your mouth!
(Susan and Sean)

Summing Up

We have talked about people in our lives, and particularly those unlikable, detestable people who we would rather ignore. We have talked about needing people in every area of our life and how to get ourselves to the point where we are comfortable with people. There had been many 'How To' Books dealing with various aspects of our working or business life and how we should get ahead. Some of the headings under which discussion has taken place in these books, include Time Management, Strategic Planning, Goal Setting, Leadership Skills, The Business Plan, Risk Taking, Brainstorming, etc. etc. While these are all excellent and worthwhile areas of expertise to study – they cannot be studied in solitary isolation. They need input from people. Whichever way you look, and what ever you want to excel in, the way ahead needs people. Without them, you are lost, so lets look for a moment and find out why.

- You are born – a product of **people.**
- You grow up – moulded by those same **people.**
- You are educated by **people** and boy, there are some Slimy Frogs in the education system.
- You go on to higher learning and are endowed with further knowledge of your subject by **people.**
- You go out to work with **people** whether you are in a company or you have your own business.
- You have a partnership with, or get married to another **person.**
- You plan and execute your entire career or careers in concert with other **people.**
- Even if you are at home, either by choice or necessity, you have **people** who are relatives, friends or acquaintances.

So I could go on, ad infinitum. Suffice it to say that people are indeed the highest priority in our lives and we have the ability to change our lives for the better if we will only give this fact the full recognition it is due. How we get on in our lives has less and less to do with systems and procedures and more and more to do with how we co-exist and deal with other people. We maintain that the biggest obstacle of all is the people we must inevitably deal with to get where we want to be and if some of those people turn out to be Slimy Frogs, we have even bigger problems. If you are not a 'people person', this dealing with people can be daunting enough for you to consider that it is not worth the effort. You, or anyone else may often opt for the status quo and familiarity rather than deal with people who start off as strangers and have to be cultivated in order to build the relationship.

Why we Need Frogs and People

Many professionals – and non-professionals for that matter – contend that many people don't get on in life because they don't get on with it – whatever their particular 'it' is. Is this a fair statement? I think not. There are many, many circumstances which govern our ability to 'get on with it', not the least of which are our own views of our self and others. Much of a person's inability to progress has to do with outside circumstances, sometimes of our own making and sometimes beyond our control. Even matters beyond our control can be dealt with, but it takes strict discipline for us to surmount those circumstances. This process involves a lot of thinking, planning, and extra tenacity together with a mountain of help and encouragement from other people.

We all dream and there is nothing wrong with dreaming. The problem for many people is turning those dreams into reality. We have our inner self to deal with and that is tough. Many self-help books and seminars present the view that 'all things are possible' – we have just to sweep aside the obstacles and 'do it'. If it were as simple as that, we would have many more successful people. Issues and circumstances which can interfere with progress on this front include other people who can unwittingly be responsible for negative influences on our lives. To free us from these people often requires radical change in our lifestyle in order to imbue ourselves with attitudes which are going to have a positive effect on our lives.

Note that we did not say 'positive' attitudes. We think that you are allowed to have any kind of attitude you like providing that a negative attitude through negative influence doesn't dominate all the time. Humanly, we cannot be positive all of the time – we have to allow ourselves the luxury of ranting, sulking, shouting or being angry or frightened. However, there is a world of difference between being this way and having a continuing negative attitude to your life.

If you dwell in an environment of negativity, you will never solve any problems because you will always permit yourself the luxury of creating new problems out of the problems you are trying to solve. Let us explain. Suppose you have a problem because you suddenly have to go to town instead of picking your partner up from work, five miles in the other direction. There are plenty of easy solutions to this, but you spend your time thinking of another excuse once you solve the one you have been working on. If the truth is to be known, you really don't want to find a solution at all. This is a symptom of a much deeper, troubled complex, which stops you from doing the things you want to do. It also provides you with a wonderful excuse not to get out and meet other people. Positive energy interspersed with negative energy will encourage you to get on with your life. All of one or all of the other will not achieve any result at all.

Another attribute which we are told contributes to our success in life is to have a 'passion to do something'; a passion to succeed in our chosen field of business, a passion to play the piano, a passion to climb mountains, to go on the stage or to travel the world. Unfortunately for many of us, we are unable to identify what we would really like to do in life, never mind develop a passion for it!

In order for us to try and discover our ideal calling, it means first of all digging deep within ourselves and exposing ourselves to different opportunities and experiences which involve the help and assistance of other people so that we may discover exactly what we might have a passion for. Passion means forgetting or ignoring every other aspect of your life in order to accommodate your passion – it means developing single mindedness.

It means being able to deal with the handicaps we have to surmount in order to be able to pursue our passion once it has been identified. These handicaps can be formidable – especially if you are a struggling single parent without two pennies to rub together and absolutely no prospect for the future. During this process, you need abundant support from a number of people, not just on an ad hoc basis, but continuously because it will be a long, hard road. You will need people, people and more people.

Perhaps, for many of us, success means being content within ourselves – to avoid confrontation and to enjoy ambling on from one day to another. We still need 'co-operative' people to help us achieve this. This contented life will certainly not be achieved if we mix with negative, unco-operative or un-likable people. This is the point where we have to decide that either we are going to learn to avoid such people, or we are going to learn to try and befriend them.

Simply, unless you are going to spend your life as a recluse or hermit, you need people. To receive the benefit from those people and what they have to offer, you need to get along with them. The more you network and contact people, the easier it will become for you to develop relationships with difficult people. We do not have to look far for an example of the benefits of this.

Returning to Chapter 1, Princess Wantalot, when finally capitulating, enjoyed the frog snogging which had repulsed her for weeks beforehand. Furthermore, although Whatsinitforme was an ugly, Slimy Frog, she found that at the point of capitulation, she and Whatsinitforme could have gone on to greater things and may well have been able to build some kind of relationship out of snogging. On the other hand, she also found that she had the power to make the Frog stick to the deal he had made and this made her feel good.

Can we draw personal parallels to this situation, or are we quite discontented in our own little world we have built around ourselves, and are too afraid to venture out of it? How many people reach the end of their lives feeling 'if only' and die in a state of regret for lost opportunities.

Most people fail to act because of fear of failure. For many it is so easy to stay with the safe company and the safe job with the guaranteed pension scheme. The greatest fear of all is snogging – in daring to go out and deal with other people. The fear is founded because there be slimy frogs out there – and few are to be trusted.

It is quite possible that during the course of your life you are going to meet someone who will have a profound and dramatic effect on your life, changing it for the better. It will be someone you are 'meant' to meet. How are you going to be able to meet that person if you are not able to avail yourself of the possibility of meeting them? In order to do this, you have to contact and snog people. If you don't, then perhaps your hopes and dreams will remain forever that – hopes and dreams.

With our need for people and contact with people, the ultimate need is to be genuine and to genuinely like these people. You cannot fake it. Faking may be successful in the short run, but somewhere along the road things will go dreadfully wrong and start to disintegrate. It is no good snogging with your mouth shut. If you are going to snog, then it has to be all the way or nothing and you can only go this route if you have the experience to do it.

We firmly believe that any relationship you have with anybody has to be 'the real thing'. This not only applies to intimate relationships, but also to friendships, acquaintanceships and business associateships. If a relationship fizzles out, it does so because there was no real nucleus there in the first place. You should never use somebody or some Frog for the time that you need them and then cast them aside. If you approach Slimy Frog with this attitude, you will find that the relationship will turn out to be like a game of chess – planned, calculating, automatic and strategised and you, not Slimy, is going to end up being check-mated. On the other hand, if you approach Slimy with the idea of winning him over as a friend, then your chances of achieving your goals through him improve considerably.

It is true that some people seem to have the luck of the Irish and the best possible Frog they could wish for simply falls into their laps without them even trying. Sadly for the rest of us, it is the night of the long snog. Luck, good fortune and opportunity is something that is worked at, it is not given free of charge and effort. If you are going to make it, you must remember that the world will not come banging on your door – you have to go out and engage with your market to achieve your goal.

Once you overcome the fear of stepping over your doorstep and if you can let yourself go, snogging can be great fun. The place to go from here is to develop a network, find a frog and get snogging. Don't hang around riddled with nerves. Don't allow self-doubt to creep in because, the moment that happens, your attention will be focused on your own nervousness. The minute you take a step across the room to introduce yourself to a potential contact, in that instant your attention

160

is drawn away from yourself to the matter in hand. Even if you make a mistake, continue on and do it – don't stop.

Having decided to take the plunge and snog, many of us find that we tend to be overly sensitive individuals who take offence at the slightest remark or action during the course of a regular conversation. We must try very hard not to do this. Step back and look at the whole perspective. We have talked about shooting ourselves in the foot and sabotaging our dreams just at the point when they will become reality.

As well as not being in control of our emotions, it can also mean over-sensitivity, an offshoot of emotion, and if we want to be successful with our Frog snogging we cannot afford that. In order to be less sensitive, we must have a secure support system of one or two people (possibly more) on whom we can count, even when the last chip is down. As long as we have this security, we can afford to overlook small remarks which we see as a threat. If someone makes a remark that you might tend to blow out of all proportion, then rein yourself in and let it go. You are not dependent upon that remark – you are dependent upon the relationship as a whole.

One of the best attributes we can have, enabling us to get along with someone else is humour. We may have been advised of this often, but how often do we apply it? The greatest gift of all is the ability to laugh at *us*.

Sharing is another issue which we tend to ignore. I went into a store once and met a lady behind the counter who was not happy. Ours was a brief contact and did not allow for any in-depth questioning of her situation, but I managed to ascertain that she did not share her problems with other people – even her husband or those closest to her.

"Why ever not?" I asked.

"Oh," she said, "I just cannot do that, I wouldn't do that." It was a limp reply which spelled volumes and I often think back to this lady and how much better her life would have been if she had been able to share and get feedback from other people. Another plus about sharing is that as you share, you develop a compassion for other people which again can help you on your Frog snogging quest.

Sharing means caring and we have to show that we care. Forget about any kind of reserve – people need you and you need them. As you snog, you learn about empathy, compassion, understanding, humour and the joy of sharing interests and what better background to take with you when you beard the lion in its den – The Slimy Frog. We offer you these four wise blessings:

1) May your Frog be well built and good-looking.

2) May your Frog be rich and generous.

3) May your Frog have the breath of an angel.

4) May your lips never become dry and cracked.

Remember:

He who snogs wins

Happy snogging
Susan Lancaster & Sean Orford

*The authors welcome your comments and invite you to contact them through their e-mail address at **frogsnogger@cs.com***